THE SILENT TRAVELLER
IN LAKELAND

THE SILENT TRAVELLER
IN LAKELAND

Chiang Yee

www.mercatpress.com

First published in 1937 by Methuen & Co

This edition published in 2004 by Mercat Press Ltd
10 Coates Crescent, Edinburgh EH3 7AL
www.mercatpress.com

Text and illustrations © Chiang Yee
Foreword © Da Zheng 2004

ISBN: 184183 0674

The essay 'A Dream of the English Lakeland' was first published in the
Journal of the Fell and Rock Climbing Club of the English lake District in 1938

Cover illustration: *Taylorgill Force in the Lake District* by Chiang Yee

Set in Galliard and Marigold at Mercat Press

Printed and bound in Great Britain by Antony Rowe Ltd

Contents

illustrations

打桨湖心来浩々波
萬頃空久胸臆涼照
波皆緑影舷外好
風吹冷然鷗夢醒

德韻特湖上遊船 山

I sail through the heart of the lake plying my oar—
On every side the leaping tops of the waves—
Sit long till my body shivers with chilliness.
All the water reflections are green shadows,
And a mild breeze blows outside round the gunwale,
Calmly awakens the seagulls from dreams.

To My Sister

Foreword

DA ZHENG

From 28 November, 1935 to 7 March, 1936, the International Exhibition of Chinese Art was held at the Royal Academy in London, displaying an unprecedented assemblage of painting, calligraphy, jade, sculpture, bronze and porcelain from China, England and several other countries. In the midst of a growing interest in Chinese art, the exhibition aroused a genuine curiosity and excitement in the public about Asian cultural history and civilization.

Among numerous publications that accompanied the Exhibition was *The Chinese Eye*, a relatively unusual book by a Chinese writer previously unknown to the public. The title of the book is a reference to the ways that the Chinese observe things, especially works of art and nature. Free of academic jargon, the book is delightfully entertaining and original. It provides a simple but deft interpretation of Chinese art from the perspective of an experienced artist, offering rare insights into the philosophical, literary and aesthetic nature of that subject. Most importantly, it underlines the vast differences between Chinese and Western tastes and practices in art. Indeed, the book was so popular that one month after its initial publication it was reprinted and a month later was released in its second edition.

The author of *The Chinese Eye* was Chiang Yee, an artist and poet who had been in England for less than three full years. Born in China in 1903, he grew up in a well-to-do family in Jiangxi, a province in the south-east known for its porcelain products. He received his elementary education at the family school, and he learned to paint and write poems at a young age. China was undergoing turbulent social and cultural changes during the first half of the twentieth century. After the feudal Manchurian government was overthrown in 1911, civil wars among warlords continued for many years. In the meantime, the nation struggled to deal with foreign powers that attempted to divide its territories for economic and political ends. As a result, Chiang went to college and majored in chemistry, in the belief that science would be instrumental in bringing about a powerful new China.

After graduation, however, he embarked on a completely different career path. He joined the Northern Expedition to fight warlords and unite the nation, and he later served as the magistrate of three districts successively, including his own hometown, Jiujiang. His fervent aspiration and youthful passion were soon crushed by the painful realisation that the political system in China was corrupt. In 1933, he left for England to study politics at the University of London, planning to return after a year or so to bring about social and economic changes in China. But a series of unexpected events extended his sojourn overseas. He joined the faculty at the School of Oriental Studies in 1935 and then worked at the Wellcome Historical Medical Museum from 1938. During World War Two, he moved to Oxford, where he stayed until 1955 when he was offered a faculty position at Columbia University in the United States. He was not able to make a return to China until 1975, after an absence of forty-two years.

Even though *The Chinese Eye* was a success, Chiang Yee could not enjoy this, for he was deeply concerned with the safety of his family in China, which was on the brink of war with Japan. Anxiety and worries about his family were gnawing at his heart all the time. In July of 1936, at his English friends' suggestion, Chiang took a trip to the Lake District, known for its associations with famous English poets and writers, such as Wordsworth, Coleridge, Southey, De Quincey and Ruskin. He had been living in London for three years, working under electric lights and walking in the smoggy and crowded atmosphere of an industrial city. He missed mountains and lakes. His previous trip to North Wales with some other tourists in the summer of 1934 had been a 'bitter disappointment', because he was not able to enjoy a moment of uninterrupted peace in order to immerse himself in nature and observe the scenery closely by himself. On 31 July, Chiang arrived at Wastwater. Over the next two weeks, he visited Derwentwater, Buttermere, Crummockwater, Windermere and Grasmere, making some sketches of the local scenes during the journey. While it seemed nearly impossible to locate a quiet spot in London, in the Lake District there had been tranquillity and peace. The journey, he noted, was 'the most agreeable period of all my English experience.'

When he returned to London on 12 August, there was a letter awaiting him. It had come from the manager of Country Life Ltd., a publisher in London. The manager had seen Chiang's painting 'Ducks in St. James's Park' in *The Illustrated London News* and wanted to meet the artist. At the meeting, he suggested that Chiang should consider writing *A Chinese Artist in London* with his own illustrations; he mentioned Yoshio Markino's *A Japanese Artist in London* (1910), which had sold very well two decades earlier. Chiang replied with a smile on his face, 'That is exactly what I have been working on.' He showed the manager the sketches and the journal he had prepared during the visit to the Lake District, which he believed could be published as a volume. The manager took the material back for consideration.

The following day, the manager of Country Life telephoned. He told Chiang that the journal was unfortunately too scanty to make a marketable volume. As for the sketches, he was afraid that few people could appreciate the Lake District in Chinese painting style.

At that time, Chiang was teaching at the School of Oriental Studies, whose library had a fair collection of travel books about China by missionaries and diplomats. Chiang had noticed, after a quick survey, that most of those books were 'unfair and irritating at times.' The writers of these books pandered to the 'unhealthy curiosity' of the West by focusing on exotic opium smokers, beggars and coolies. Some of the authors did not really know China. They had been there for only a few months and could not even read or speak Chinese. Nevertheless, these writings had sold well, and only helped spread prejudice and misconceptions. It occurred to Chiang that he should write about what he had seen in England 'on the principle of looking for similarities among all kinds of people, not their differences or their oddities.'

He submitted the manuscript to Methuen, which had published his book *The Chinese Eye*, but he got a rejection immediately. He then tried several other publishers and was turned down one after another. To get published was an onerous task for an unknown writer; more so for a non-English writer.

Surprisingly enough, the manager of Country Life called six months later to check on the progress of the London book. Chiang insisted that he would not write a book on London unless the Lake District book was published first. A month later, the manager came to inform him that the publisher 'had decided to take the risk of publishing the slight book on the English Lakeland, with one condition—no royalty', except for six complimentary copies. Chiang accepted the offer. The following week, at the signing of the contract, an unexpected obstacle emerged: the publisher refused to accept the proposed title *The Silent Traveller in Lakeland* because the phrase 'The Silent Traveller', which was Chiang's pen-name, sounded 'sinister' and could provoke suspicions from Scotland Yard. Chiang argued that the precaution was unnecessary. He explained that such a title would only help the sale. Eventually, they reached a compromise by affixing a subtitle to it: *The Silent Traveller: A Chinese Artist in Lakeland*.

In the Autumn of 1937, the book was published with a short preface by the art critic Herbert Read. He commended Chiang's earlier book *The Chinese Eye* for introducing the West to the Chinese conception of art in a lucid and comprehensible manner. In this Lake District book, according to Read, Chiang proves that Chinese art is 'not bound by geographical limits; it is universal, and can interpret... English landscape just as well as the Chinese landscape.' Chiang's endeavour, much the same as Wordsworth's, is to show 'the universality of all true modes of feeling and thinking. The relationship of man to his environment is the relationship of two constants—earth the same and man the same, eternally. What is inconstant is man's ability to seize and express the real nature of that relationship.'

To some extent, the Lake District book is a record of Chiang's exploration and discovery of this 'universality' and the two 'constants' that Read has mentioned. Chiang used to believe that English scenery was 'set against a background of sea' and 'somehow different from home.' This journey to the Lake District, however, enabled him to see 'how similar Nature is everywhere.' The waterfalls, trees, mountains, rocks and clouds, all seemed so familiar, reminding him of his homeland and allowing him to compare and contrast the two. He came to perceive that 'nature has never changed to me in moving from place to place; she differs only according to my changing states of mind.'

In the book, Chiang never attempts to hide his racial and ethnic identity. Rather, he celebrates his identity as a manifestation of otherness while playfully undermining the arbitrary barrier that separates the East from the West. He appears idiosyncratic in his preferences: he enjoys walking rather than taking the automobile; he wants to stay alone rather than enjoying the company of a friend; he prefers to face the natural scene directly rather than consulting the printed tourist books. Yet he is quick to persuade his Western audience of the logic behind these idiosyncrasies. In Derwentwater, for example, he chooses to rest by the road rather than to move restlessly like other tourists. To passers-by, this 'poor Chinese' might appear laughable, yet he is actually taking pleasure in admiring the picturesque scenic beauty that other 'so-called Nature-lovers' have missed: he views distant Skiddaw 'as if she were a noble lady of Elizabethan times sitting there with her robes and draperies widely spread around her of purplish and brown colour, and shining in the reflection of the setting sun.' Boating is another case in point. Chiang and his Chinese friend's seemingly unorthodox method of controlling the boat—with the rower sitting facing the front—appears foolish, but Chiang offers his own practical and aesthetic reasons for the arrangement. In short, Chiang's Chinese identity allows him to gain a unique vantage point from which to comment on Western culture, and he is able to draw out differences in similarities— and similarities in differences—between the East and West.

In *The Silent Traveller*, Chiang includes thirteen plates of his own creation, each of which contains a painting above one or two poems executed in Chinese calligraphy, an exotic but unique artistic feature of this book. All these plates are monochromatic, using only black ink, with the effect of light and darkness depending on the varied speed of the Chinese brush and the quantity of water on the absorbent paper. While these paintings are unmistakably Chinese (though they somewhat resemble watercolour), a reader, struck by the similarity between a black-and-white photograph of another

English scene and a painting by Chiang, marvelled at the sharp observation of the Oriental painter in catching the mood of those scenes generally overlooked by the Westerner. 'I never remember seeing any such scene by an English watercolourist, yet it must be common enough in Autumn', he exclaimed.

Despite the superficial resemblances, Chiang's monochrome paintings essentially differ from black-and-white photographs because of the 'Chinese Eye', a unique perspective of the Chinese artist on Western culture. A camera presents the scene through its lens mechanically, but a Chinese painter observes, selects, and restructures the world with his brush and ink. As one of the very few pioneers who attempt to represent the Western world in a traditional Chinese art form, Chiang, as exemplified in his *Silent Traveller* series, has been one of the most daring and original in his experimentation with and expansion of technique and subject-matter. However, unlike the illustrations in his subsequent *Silent Traveller* books which depict Western architecture, city scenes and city dwellers, those in this Lake District book are all landscape paintings, with trees, mountains, rivers and farm houses that are nearly indistinguishable from their counterparts in traditional paintings in China. Chiang tentatively explores the new possibility of representing familiar elements in this totally strange place. Even the plate 'Going to Church in the rain, Wasdale Head', which is the only plate in the book that includes human figures, may easily be mistaken for a rain scene in China. Because of the limitations as well as the possibilities of the Chinese brush, and because of the Chinese art tradition, Chiang must have discovered some comfortable congeniality in the landscapes of the Lake District as a companion as well as an artistic subject.

The artistic tradition that shaped Chiang's representation emphasises an economy of expression in bringing the truth out of nature. Ancient philosophers in China passionately speculated on this subject of representation; they believed that physical resemblance was only secondary to the artistic and emotional expression of the self. *Lao-tzu*, a Taoist text, begins with a statement related to this paradox: 'A Way about which we can make statements is not the Constant Way.' In other words, nature is independent of either literary or artistic language, and language, an autonomous system that leads to perception and knowledge, only blocks and distorts our knowledge of nature. Due to this limitation, as Stephen Owen has suggested, 'when utilizing language, we are operating within its boundaries.' For the same reason, colour, light, and even form are considered transient and thus unimportant in Chinese art, so their representation often appears unrealistic. Unlike a photograph, a landscape painting does not often resemble the actual scene in nature, yet such a representation can paradoxically be more truthful since it aims to reach for the essence of nature. As Chiang comments, 'Our Chinese artist tries to paint the Nature in his mind, not the Nature in Nature, and so his pictures do not search for exact resemblance. Nevertheless, resemblance is inherent in his work, for it derives from genuine natural impressions.' In these plates, Chiang omits many details in the landscape and nearly all human figures, a practice that substantiates Chiang's claim that the shapes of the geographical topology, the overall impression, and the suggestiveness of the absent objects in the artwork are quintessential.

Interestingly enough, the artistic presentation of the Lake District through the 'Chinese Eye' corresponds with Wordsworth's theory of representation. Wordsworth insists that the true artist should have the freedom to record his imaginative reactions to and conceptions of nature. Only such a recording would serve the primary aim of rendering the 'essential truth' of the given scene. To Wordsworth, imagination is a subjective term because 'it deals with objects not as they are, but as they appear to the mind of the poet.' He advocates that the painter should give 'reverent attention on all that surrounded him' when taking a walk and should use the picture that survives in his mind some days later, which contains the 'ideal and essential truth of the scene.' Wordsworth's poetics is similar to the theory of the traditional Chinese art of emphasising the essence rather than the external forms of the matter.

Except for a few passages that discuss moral issues and current political situations, *The Silent Traveller in Lakeland* carries a light and tranquil tone. The apparent serenity, contrasting with the hideous crisis looming ahead, recalls the nerve-racking horror masked by intense, explosive stillness in Hemingway's 'Hills Like White Elephants' or 'The Big Two-Hearted River'. On 27 July, 1936, four days before Chiang's journey to the Lake District, the Spanish Civil War began. The rebels bombed Malaga, killing a number of innocent civilians. Violence and brutality disrupted the relatively peaceful rhythm of life after the First World War, and a new war seemed inevitable in Europe. The unstable situation exerted an immense psychological impact on Chiang, whose homeland in the East had been invaded by the Japanese and whose family had been forced to evacuate and relocate.

Chiang's lengthy discussion of the War at his breakfast table on 6 August is the exact middle point of his journey, and it becomes symbolically the climax of the narrative. Chiang questions modern concepts such as progress, civilisation and religion, as he points out that the war has a devastating impact on art. For that very reason, the Lake District, sacred and sublime, holds a special meaning to Chiang: it is a protective, replenishing and holy enclave. Yet this peaceful atmosphere is, in reality, so delicate and fragile that it could easily be shattered and vanish. Chiang refuses to read the newspaper for fear that the news coverage of the war could effect a ravaging disturbance to the delicate peace in the Lake District.

In fact, the sanctuary is on the verge of extinction. In addition to the war on the continent, there are multiple threats from other causes, such as industrialisation, commercialism and tourism. The railways and railway stations are constructed, the noise of the automobile jars the soothing sound of pines, and the motorboat frightens the fish and birds on the lake. A 'big, square, stolid hotel with bright yellow painted walls' stands on the hillside, conspicuously out of place in the surrounding natural scene. In Windermere, outside the home of Wordsworth, Chiang is alarmed by the swarms of tourists who come not to enjoy the beauty of nature but to take photos of the house to satisfy their vanity. Seeing the rows of cars and the multitudes of tourists, Chiang laments, 'We are back in London again.' Glaring capitalism has defiled moral and aesthetic sense as well as altered the configuration of nature. Even the native gardener, tempted by the 'marvellous' town life, is no longer content with his profession. Chiang is utterly sarcastic when asserting that Wordsworth must have been 'an unintentional philanthropist', for he has provided so many jobs and so much for the 'interest of visitors' who have scarcely any taste for scenery. In short, the original Lake District that inspired Wordsworth has vanished, giving way to a commercialised tourist attraction.

The concluding poem 'On Leaving Lakeland', a six-line regular verse, brings the journey to a seemingly satisfactory denouement.

> In my native country, there is the Mountain Lu,
> It rises too beside the P'o-Yang Lake.
> And my home stands upon its shore,
> All night, and day, I see the changing colour of the
> mountain.
> I leave this Lakeland, and with longing seek to return,
> With some sadness thoughts are born of my distant
> home!

The three couplets of the poem indicate the three stages in a progressive unfolding of Chiang's emotions. The first one stresses the equally beautiful setting of Chiang's own hometown in China. The word 'too' connects Lu Mountain and the P'o-Yang Lake with the Lake District in England. Having arrived there, the 'homesick Easterner' travels back in time to his past in the second couplet; and upon leaving, he plans to return in the future while remembering his homeland with some sadness.

A comparison between this poem and the following one by Tao Yuanming (AD 365-427), a great Jin poet, could help to highlight not just how both of these poets search for a rural idyll but also how the ancient poet is invoked by the diasporic Chinese poet of the modern world to soothe his yearning to return home in entirely different cultural and historical conditions.

> I built my hut beside a travelled road
> Yet hear no noise of passing carts and horses.
> You would like to know how it is done?
> With the mind detached, one's place becomes remote.
> Picking chrysanthemums by the eastern hedge
> I catch sight of the distant southern hills:
> The mountain air is lovely as the sun sets
> And flocks of flying birds return together.
> In these things is a fundamental truth
> I would like to tell, but lack the words.[1]

Tao Yuanming, born in the same county as Chiang Yee, also served as the magistrate of various districts in Jiangxi. A man of strong inclination for freedom and dignity, Tao chose to retire and become a recluse rather than having to tolerate the official life in which he found himself constantly forced to compromise his principles. Influenced by the Discursive Poetry of the early Jin, a philosophical school concerned about the harmonious relationship between humans and nature, Tao built a hut in an inhabited area, enjoying peace in the noisy human world. Simple activities, such as 'picking

1 Tse-tsung Chou, ed. Wen-lin: *Studies in the Chinese Humanities* (Madison: University of Wisconsin Press, 1968), p. 12.

chrysanthemums by the eastern hedge' and viewing 'the distant southern hills,' became a means for him to search for the 'fundamental truth.' Tao differed from his contemporaries in that, while others were busy searching for 'truth' in excursions and conversations, Tao discovered 'truth' in the daily activities and natural objects around him. His poems on his retired life have become known as 'farmland poetry,' and he has been regarded as the predecessor of 'hermit poets.'

In addition to the obvious similarities in linguistic, thematic, and descriptive aspects between these two poems, there is a critical connection through the common usage of the Chinese phrase *youran*, an attitude that Discursive Poetry and later landscape poetry generally share. In Chiang's poem, this term is rendered as 'with some sadness.' It goes well with the English version that Chiang has provided to his readers in the West, but the rendition has left out the other possible meaning of the phrase, totally different in tempo and tone: leisure, pleasure, tastefulness, as well as distance. To Chiang, the homeward journey itself, rather than the journey's ultimate destination, assumes primary importance. Unlike Tao, Chiang cannot possibly undertake a journey back to Lu Mountain; even if it were feasible, he would only confront a war-torn hometown, debauched by Japanese invaders. Staying in the West makes him a perpetual sojourner and a dreamer of home(land), with 'a certain gilding of romanticism.' While Tao is able to 'catch sight of the distant southern hills,' such a view not only enables him to be detached and his moral integrity uncontaminated by the world, but also provides what Robert Hightower claims is the 'bridge between preoccupation and perception'. Nevertheless, Chiang, being an exiled Chinese in the West, can perceive the 'Southern Hills' or Lu Mountain only in his imagination. The medium—either language or art—becomes the means to re-vive, re-present, and re-invent a remote past that he can identify with. The multiple meanings denoted by the phrase *youran*—'with some sadness,' 'leisurely,' and 'distantly'—are all applicable to Chiang's poem, orchestrating a dream-like undertone of nostalgia.

To everybody's great surprise, Chiang's book on the Lake District was again a huge success. Its first edition sold out in a month, and the manager of the publishing company telephoned the author and offered a reprint. 'Times have changed,' he proclaimed; Chiang replied, 'My thoughts have also changed. I want a normal royalty for the second edition.' Since then nine editions have been published, and this slim volume has become the first of the Silent Traveller series. Chiang wrote thirteen travel books, covering his travel experiences in Europe, Asia, Australia and America.

Chiang revisited the Lake District not long after. This was a fascinating experience recorded in his essay 'A Dream of the English Lakeland,' published in *The Journal of the Fell and Rock Climbing Club* in 1938. It is a wonderful companion piece, complementing and underlining some of the thematic, emotional, and aesthetic aspects of *The Silent Traveller*.

As one of the few celebrated Chinese writers in the English language in the twentieth century, Chiang Yee's writing has influenced thousands of people in the West. His travel writing has helped the West to understand the East, to perceive the beauty of nature, and to see the commonalities among all peoples in the world. Although many readers today may be new to his works, they will inevitably be intrigued and enchanted by the wit and fresh insights in his writings. He has a distinct voice, and his messages are still relevant when he addresses the need for peace, for mutual respect, and for a world of harmony.

Boston, Massachusetts, April 2004

Preface

HERBERT READ

Mr Chiang Yee is a master of the art of landscape painting. Those who are already familiar with his work have accepted it as the modern expression of a national tradition. That is to say, we have regarded it as specifically Chinese painting, and we have been grateful to Mr Chiang in particular because in his earlier book, *The Chinese Eye*, he has explained the Chinese conception of art so clearly and thus enabled us to appreciate its qualities with a true aesthetic understanding. But we still thought of Chinese art as something with a Chinese content—Chinese mountains, Chinese lakes, Chinese trees. But now the artist comes forward as if to say: 'My vision, my technique, in short, my art is not bound by geographical limits; it is universal, and can interpret your English landscape just as well as the Chinese landscape.'

We English are rather sensitive about our landscape. We have our own great tradition of landscape painting, and we have a great landscape poetry. We might legitimately feel that painters like Constable, Turner, Crome, Girtin, Cotman, and many others of their school, have depicted the very spirit of our hills and streams, our meadows and villages. No less legitimately we might claim that our poets—Shakespeare,

Thomson, Gray, Collins, Wordsworth, Keats and Tennyson—have created a unique poetry of landscape, so intimate and true that there is nothing left to celebrate, no nuance of form or feeling that has escaped their intuitive apprehension.

But Mr Chiang, who is a poet as well as a painter, has dared to enter our national shrine and to worship there in his own way. He has taken his pen and his brush and has written a book and painted a series of landscapes which challenge our complacency. He has gone to the very holy of holies of our nature poets—to the Lake District—and has followed in the footsteps of the great prophets of our cult, Wordsworth and Ruskin. In his direct way he has proved what some years ago I ventured to assert as a paradox—the nearness of Wordsworth's poetry to certain oriental modes of feeling and thinking. But we must abandon these geographical and nationalistic comparisons. What Mr Chiang shows, no less clearly than Wordsworth, is the universality of all true modes of feeling and thinking. The relationship of man to his environment is the relationship of two constants—earth the same and man the same, eternally. What is inconstant is man's ability to seize and express the real nature of that relationship.

> Oh! mystery of man, from what a depth
> Proceed thy honours. I am lost, but see
> In simple childhood something of the base
> On which thy greatness stands; but this I feel,
> That from thyself it comes, that thou must give
> Else never canst receive.

This "simple childhood" which Wordsworth realised as fundamental to any greatness in humanity is also the innocent and incorruptible vision of the poet and the painter. It is the vision which Mr Chiang has brought to our beloved lakes and mountains, whose subtle essence he expresses with such fidelity.

湖匪畫記

i

Introduction

There are numbers of books on travel and scenery published every year, some of them written from the geologist's special point of view, some to dilate upon peculiar racial differences, and some purely for the sake of an unusual piece of scenery, or of some lovable romantic incident that happened there. But the book I am about to write is unlike any of these!

The English Lakes are familiar by name to everyone who knows England at all or has ever stayed in that country, although he may never have visited the Lakes themselves. The reason lies, I think, not with their special geological interest, certainly not a sociological one, or even ultimately with the character of their scenery. The Lakes are known through the fame of their poets. William Wordsworth is the giant among them, whose reputation has travelled even to the Far East; we Chinese, whether English scholars or not, have opportunities of reading his poems, for collections of them have been translated, and many of us indeed find them appealing very closely to our sensibility. There are discoverable among them some elements in common with our own great masters of natural description. Those of us who come to

England make Stratford-upon-Avon an object of pilgrimage, but with an equal unanimity we determine also to visit the Lakes, and especially Grasmere, where Wordsworth spent a good part of his life.

Thomas De Quincey wrote some remarks about the early upbringing of Wordsworth in relation to his character:

> I do not conceive that Wordsworth could have been an amiable boy; he was austere and unsocial, I have reason to think, in his habits; not generous; and self-denying... Wordsworth, like his companions, haunted the hills and the vales for the sake of angling, snaring birds, swimming, and sometimes of hunting, according to the Westmorland fashion (or the Irish fashion in Galway), on foot; for the riding to the chase is quite impossible, from the precipitous nature of the ground. It was in the course of these pursuits, by an indirect effect growing gradually upon him, that Wordsworth became a passionate lover of nature, at the time when the growth of his intellectual faculties made it possible that he should combine thoughtful passions with the experience of the-eye and the ear... Wordsworth, though not idle as regarded his own pursuits, was so as regarded the pursuits of the place.

(From the *Reminiscences of the English Lake Poets.*)

This illustrates to what extent the beautiful surroundings of the Lake district during his boyhood made Wordsworth great; but, on the other hand, I think Wordsworth has made known the greatness of the Lakes, anyway to us—people of China.

Last summer I had the opportunity of visiting the Lakes, and there I spent the most agreeable period of all my English experience. So happy was that stretch of time that, even now, I often drive back my imagination to the weeks I spent there and the loveliness of the spots I visited; then I re-write some of the verses I roughly composed there, and make sketches from scenes stored up in my mind. I cannot analyse the peculiar beauty of those places, but though I believe there can be no fundamental difference in natural scenery all over the world—rocks, hills, mountain-peaks, streams and waterfalls everywhere have a common character—yet I was constantly aware of some half-likeable, half-melancholy strangeness, reminding me that this was not my native country. For these last three years I have been living under London fogs, and as the time passes I feel very conscious of growing old; this happy moment of time which I spent in the Lakes brings me particular joy by comparison, and it may be that I think of those places in retrospect with a certain gilding of romanticism. This small book may turn out to be a rather unusual presentation of lake scenery, from the point of view of a homesick Easterner.

Since I was born at the foot of Lu Mountain, one of China's most famous mountains, from my earliest childhood I grew up in the companionship of rocks, hills, mountain-peaks, streams, waterfalls, pines and every kind of tree. While I was among them I quite forgot the existence of towns and cities. The musical murmuring of the drifting streams, the drizzling of rain on the leaves, and their beautiful fresh green afterwards, the clouds steadily rising up from the valleys to the peaks, the mists hiding distant villages and tree-tops—all of these made me tireless of wandering, and brought a great tranquillity of spirit; I seemed to feel my breath coming deeper and longer while face to face with them. As I grew older, I had, of course, to spend some time in schools and offices, but I was never long in returning to the mountains.

We have a phrase in Chinese which translated literally means, 'The fee for mountains and rivers,' and is a synonym for 'travelling expenses.' It is a clear enough indication of the nature of my country—it abounds in water and mountains; if you want to travel from place to place, you cannot help meeting them. I was fortunate indeed in finding them everywhere, for I have travelled over most parts of my huge country. I never grew tired of looking at mountains and rivers, for in each locality they wear a varied form; one has only to look at our landscape paintings to realise this.

Three years ago, when I was coming over to England, my impression of Nature suffered a change, for here before my eyes day after day was nothing but ocean water. On reaching Ceylon, we went ashore at Colombo, and having seen the name advertised of 'Mount Lavinia,' I eagerly hastened there. But this was no true mountain: I can remember the scene still; a small hill covered with palm trees, whose feet were washed by the sea waves—very different from the friends of my childhood.

After I had stayed in London for some time, I grew weary of traffic—the noise of buses and cars; weary of the shops rigged out day after day in their gaudy colours; of the people pushing and hurrying in the streets. Most of the time working under electric light and walking in a smoky and foggy atmosphere, I could not help feeling a growing distaste for this environment, and I suppose most Londoners have a similar experience. But one has to endure such things if one is bound to find a living among them. There are many sides of life in which the natural demands of the West have produced a higher degree of achievement than in my own country; I am thinking particularly of scientific pursuits, such as astronomy, physics, health training, etc. I also think of the peculiarly English invention of the 'week-end' which allows Londoners to get away for a short interval. We had no such term in China until very recent years. It is a good institution for a rest, and for health's sake, but it is not enough for the profound enjoyment of Nature.

The first summer I had in England I decided to join a party of holiday-makers who were visiting a place on the borders of North Wales. There, indeed, I could look upon Snowdon, Swallow Falls, and some of the typical Welsh hills, which struck me as entirely like a commonplace scene along the south bank of the Yangtze River; but as I was in a party I was obliged to follow them here, there, and everywhere, and it left me very little time to look at the surroundings as we were walking. All the members of the party were very kind to me and from my lack of conversation they seemed to conclude I was rather lonely, so they frequently came to me and offered their help with the historical background or some legends and stories surrounding this spot or the other; this kind of explanation continued unceasingly as we were on the march. (We were more than forty, and as we walked through the passes we really seemed like part of an army.) I was sincerely grateful to them and could not reject their kindness in telling me all these things; but, in fact, I am a man of curious temperament who prefers on most occasions to be dumb. When I was obliged to talk I found my tongue grow curling and painful. None of my friends realised my predicament, for I made efforts to talk easily in case they would drop their friendship with me altogether. It is a selfish trait in my character which I try to master. Whenever I walk or travel I am generally silent; I like to observe the scenery closely, and sometimes I lose all consciousness of myself in it. At such times there is no room in my mind for the external trimmings of history or romance. This habit, I must assure you, is a personal one, and not a general characteristic among my countrypeople. So it happened that my excursion to North Wales was a bitter disappointment to me, although at rare moments I had a glimpse of the familiar spirit of mountains and streams.

Some time later I had thoughts of going to see the English Lakes and Scottish Highlands. Up till last summer I had been so occupied with work that the opportunity never presented itself, but now, at last, I was free for a little while and, despite pessimistic warnings about the wet climate and the difficulties of finding lodging, I was filled with joy at the prospect of meeting my old friends—the mountains and waters. After my last experience I was determined to go alone this time; the old proverb 'Two's company...' does not hold true in my case; it would be difficult for me to find any second person who could walk with me and would be happy if I did not talk. All my friends, even my own countrymen, who can perhaps understand me better, constantly advise me not to persist in this isolation, and though I am aware it may be a bad principle, for the time being I cannot avoid it. I was almost entirely silent for a whole fortnight in the Lakes, and the joy born out of that tranquillity in my mind will render unforgettable my years in England. Before I set out I never burdened myself with studying guide books and maps of Lakeland, a duty that seems to compel many people; I rarely remember the names of places, and never the number of miles between them. Now that I have been there I burden myself unceasingly with imaginary revisitings.

湖匪畫記

ii

Wastwater

I reached Wasdale Head on the evening of July 31st, 1936, and it was Wastwater that gave me my first impression of Lakeland. First of all I should say that I had no clear picture of what to expect in the Lake District; my chief feeling about foreign scenery up till that time had been that it was somehow different from home and often set against a background of sea. From an English friend of mine who imagined that I should enjoy a rocky and wild scene I obtained the address of a lodging in Wasdale Head.

As I had anticipated, since the summer was getting hot and the time very near to August Bank Holiday, when I arrived at Euston Station half-an-hour ahead of time, the Lake Express was already packed with holiday-makers and I could hardly find a seat. I spent an entirely silent journey of seven hours. Suddenly I noticed a station board bearing the name 'Seascale,' where I was to alight. I got down hurriedly. It was a very tiny station—on one side the vast and mighty sea was clearly visible and on the other a long, curving road sloping downwards led my eye on to the furthest point of sight, where it lost itself in a dark misty grove. There was no sign of any mountain in the surroundings, except that the small station building was perched on a mound by the side of the railway line, and beside the station was a big, square, stolid hotel with bright yellow painted walls. It did not strike me as a very beautiful ornament to that particular piece of land, unless the visitors were specially anxious to have an extensive view round all four sides. No other buildings could be seen in the neighbourhood, which puzzled me at first. The great contrast of the remote white sea and the dark grove on both sides in the drizzling twilight reminded me of a painting by Whistler.

It was about eight o'clock when the train stopped at the station. There were only three passengers, including myself, who got down there. The other two were met immediately by a car waiting for them outside. I crossed a small bridge and found nobody. I was expecting to be met by someone from the lodgings, for I had made arrangements with the landlady beforehand. The wind grew fiercer and fiercer and the rain fell down in torrents. I was driven in and crouched by a corner of the station-house door, with my hat pulled over my ears and my overcoat swathed round my body, as if I were a wounded soldier from the battlefield waiting for the train to return behind the lines. Later I learned from a car owner that my lodging in Wasdale Head was thirteen miles away, so I hired his car and drove through the gathering darkness and rain. The mountains and trees were almost hidden by the dusk and mists, and I could see little through the window of the car. But even though I was moving quickly, and in a noisy mechanical contrivance, after drawing deep breaths of the mountain air, I seemed to feel myself expanding. I could not describe my feeling exactly at that time, but I certainly had sensations different from any I had experienced before. In the first place, I felt that the mountains and trees were running away from me in the opposite direction as fast as I attempted to drive nearer them. It was a different style of travelling from the old ways of my childhood in China; I often used to imagine that the mountains were ordering their trees to welcome me by nodding their heads in the wind. But here they were not so friendly, to my first reception at least, although they might welcome me more kindly the next day. Secondly, I was aware of the clear isolated sound of the motor-car, which I had never thought of hearing before, and linked with that I was delighted at the sound of pines blown by the wind and of water running under a bridge. This kind of combination would be impossible to find among the Chinese mountains. And finally, I felt that I was being brought to an unimaginable world just at that special moment, after I had endured London fogs for so long.

On arriving at my destination, the landlady seemed not to have expected me today; though the welcome was not warm I was attracted by the appearance of her small farmhouse, totally different from the Chinese ones, especially after my long stay in the town. The landlady provided me with a simple supper and a candle to light me to bed. I was tired by the journey and, after eating, lay down on my farm-bed by candle light. My only thought at that time was the joy I was to have on the morrow, meeting my old friends—the mountains and waters. I could hardly keep my eyes open to look at the ceiling of the room.

August 1st. Having arranged with the landlady to have an early breakfast, I set out from the house about a quarter to eight in the morning. I felt bewildered, not knowing which turning to take, for the landlady had given me no clear directions; but I soon discovered that this little farmhouse was situated at the bottom of a high mountain called Yewbarrow; Kirkfell lay to the left, Lingmell rose in front and Great Gable further to the left; the Screes and Wastwater were rather farther away to the right.

It was a delightful small farmhouse and might have come from some of Constable's paintings. To the left side there was a small hut, where I noticed a young girl, whom I learned to be the landlady's young sister, just feeding the hens and chickens. Her reddish face and red-coloured skirt made a vivid picture under the dark-green-leafed chestnut tree, with a remote mountain for its background. I could not help looking at her easy and innocent way of carrying out her duty.

The early morning air was still and fresh after the rain of last night, and the mountain mists were shifting from the valleys up to the mountain peaks. Suddenly a shaft of sunshine pierced the clouds and sent its rays into the valley below; from the mountain footpath where I was standing, between Lingmell and Great Gable, that sunlit valley looked far, far away. I gazed and gazed, wondering idly what lay on the other side. For the moment I was no longer a stranger, no longer the same person who had been living in London; I seemed to be back in my own country. And yet there was some intangible difference in the scene. In a short time, all the mists cleared and every mountain top appeared radiant with sunshine. But at that time they were less beautiful in my eyes than before—their whole form had become too apparent—no secret loveliness could be guessed at. My tranquillity of mind was finally disturbed by a group of cows, led by a cowherd, passing close by my side; they were all staring at me as if they knew that I was unfamiliar. Alas! I realised sharply that I did not belong to this countryside. In my own country I had seen many a time a young boy or girl riding securely on the back of a buffalo, as it plodded steadily along the edge of a rice field in the early morning and evening.

After having watched this scene, I decided to take a turn to the right and walk along the main road that lay in that direction, imagining that this would be the most beautiful part of all. I strolled along, listening to the running water cascading down from the higher reaches of the mountains, and watching the sheep here and there nibbling at the grass; it was so early that the road was still deserted. I took my fill of these things, imagining once more that I was indeed back in China. Then I came upon Wastwater—it was flat like the surface of a mirror, with the Screes soaring up behind in garments of purple and brown and the sun shining upon them. From all the things I saw at that time and heard, I began to think of the poem written by Christopher North; it seemed an exact description of this scene:

> Is this the lake, the cradle of the storms,
> Where silence never tames the mountain-roar,
> Where poets fear their self-created forms,
> Or sunk in trance severe their God adore?
> Is this the lake for ever dark and loud,
> With wave and tempest, cataract and cloud?
> Wondrous O Nature, is thy sovereign power,
> That gives to horror hours of peaceful mirth;
> For here might beauty build her summer bower!
> Lo! Where yon rainbow spans the smiling earth,
> And clothed in glory, through a silent shower,
> The mighty sun comes forth, a god-like birth;
> While 'neath his loving eye the gentle lake,
> Lies like a sleeping child too blest to wake!

My own feelings corresponded completely with this poet's thought, and from this point my own mind caught fire, and I began to think of a poem myself, which was completed afterwards.

I looked again and again at the calm water and the clear-cut outline of the Screes against the sky; it was here that I thought of making the painting which is reproduced in Plate I, although in fact it was painted indoors afterwards. I treated this entirely in Chinese manner with our own media—brush, ink and soft paper. Our style of painting inclines to bring out the subjective mood of the painter towards the scenery itself, but does not impose a stringent law on representation. I hope my readers will not be prejudiced by the traditional English landscape painting and exclaim that 'This is not like the place.'

I can vouch for anyone who had examined this spot carefully recognising it again from my picture! We very seldom use colours to enliven the painting and generally leave blank spaces to suggest water and sky. Please look at the illustration with a discerning eye!

After, I walked on a little further, and looking down on the same scene from a stone bridge my impression produced another painting. Keeping on my way, I came upon the double peak of Middle Fell; suddenly I felt a wave of familiarity—its form had great resemblance with the 'Shuang-Chien Feng' (Double-Sword Peak) of Lu Mountain in my native city. For the moment I felt a little homesick. In a short while a cloud came slowly out from the valley and mist obscured the whole view, which left with me the exact image of a painting done in Mi Yu-Jen's style (Plate II).

It was almost eleven o'clock, yet I had seen no other people on the road; glancing here and there at the splendours of Nature, I began to feel entirely 'at home' and to moralise as follows:

'In every part of the world Nature exists and has the same manifestations and yet the human face and language differ widely from place to place. Without such differences I really believe there might be peace through the whole world! But people nowadays tend to neglect Nature—to ignore her as if she never existed, eager only for the life of towns. Trains burst through the mountains in vast tunnels, mines throw up their ugly black refuse everywhere, bombs destroy the beautiful shapes of crags and trees, aeroplanes break into the solitudes.' The horrible word 'WAR' blazed itself upon my mind and destroyed every thought...

After I raised my head, I realised that mountains and trees were thick in mist—not a mountain-top could be seen; the Screes seemed to have lost their heads. I remembered being told that one could seldom tell the true height of mountains in Wasdale because their peaks were so continually covered in cloud. Then it began to rain... I walked on and on in the rain, smiling and making friends with the particles of mist as they touched my face. Although I had brought no umbrella or mackintosh with me, the custom of nearly every English inhabitant, but one to which I was not yet used, I hardly noticed that my clothes were quickly becoming soaked through; I was happy in the rain and preferred the misty mountains and trees. It was quite a different thing from walking through the slush of Piccadilly Circus or Oxford Street on a wet day in London!

I came next to a part thick with trees on both sides of the road, and a gateway with a little wooden door. About twenty yards before I reached this gateway, I turned to gaze backwards at the misty, rainy mountains, and to impress their forms very deeply into my mind. There were four youngsters playing about beside the gate; they looked surprised at my foreign appearance and, staring at me, opened the gate to let me pass through. I thanked them, and with those words broke my long silence for the first time. I stood in the woods and gazed at the Screes for a little while; they seemed to have changed colour altogether.

As I went on my way, a postman riding towards me on a bicycle wished me 'Good morning,' and I gave him 'Good morning' back. Then I came to a house called Wasdale Hall Lodge; there was a gardener clearing the path before the house, so I walked up to have a chat with him and asked him the names of the mountains. These he told me, and went on to describe his birthplace and occupation; he had apparently been born near Whitehaven, which was not very far distant from the birthplace of Wordsworth, and had worked at this lodge for about eleven years. I wondered to myself whether he could enjoy the beauty of his natural surroundings still, as I had been doing this morning—fresh to everything. In our traditional way of thought, the cowherd or woodcutter can be a very decorative addition to the beauty of Nature as well as providing a good part of a design for weaving into a landscape painting. We imagine that they may be able to enjoy themselves in some way but still can hardly fuse themselves into their natural surroundings although they have been familiar to them every day of their lives. That gardener might therefore be thinking how marvellous it must be to live in town. Alas! no one can be really content with his proper position!

The next place I reached was Santon Bridge, which consisted of an inn, a small shop marked 'Post-Office,' and a handful of houses. I walked over to the side of the stream which flowed beneath the bridge and listened to its trickling sound for quite a long while. Three boys came near me, but we did not talk to each other. It began to pour with rain, and every side of the sky blackened; it was really a fine subject for my brush, and I received an unforgettable impression for a study of stormy Nature. I tried to paint this as you see in the Frontispiece. In England, Turner is specially known for his misty and foggy compositions. In China, Mi Fei created a new style for painting misty and rainy scenes, and it is well known by the name of 'Mi-dot.' Shih-Tao also marvellously mastered his ink and used an obscure manner for painting rain and storm. I produced this painting entirely from Chinese media and used neither Mi's nor Shih-Tao's technique in it. It was painted purely from the joy of recollecting that happy instant.

About half an hour after I had reached Santon Bridge the sky cleared and the rain stopped. I walked over to lean on a wall and ate my sandwiches. Just at that spot I was really intoxicated by the scenery—mountains with clear mist behind; water rushing down the lower slopes. From time to time cars and groups of 'hikers' broke upon my dreaming, and brought me back to 'town' out of that great tranquillity.

I began walking back to Gosforth, and from there to Wasdale Head, reaching home at about 6.30 in the evening. The backward journey gave me little pleasure, for the scenery was less beautiful than before, or so it seemed, perhaps through tiredness or psychological reaction, and I was continually irritated by the noisy clamour of passing cars. When night came, I felt deeply content with my day's wanderings, but there was still a feeling of unfamiliarity in my mind. After some thought, I realised that the bareness of both lake and mountain constituted this difference; there were no lotus or water lilies floating on the surface of the water—not even a single boat sailing. And on the mountain side there were no twisted pines as I had grown accustomed to in my own country, and not a cicada droning in the trees, as their custom is with us in summer time. As a whole, Wastwater is beautiful in itself, but in some way it is a little too simple and plain for my taste, because I prefer a scene with a vast distant view or something hidden behind the trees left for imagination as in most of our Chinese landscape paintings. But at least I had thoroughly enjoyed my excursion and I had managed to forget what was going on in London. While I sat in the corner of the rather dark hall, half-lit with the flickering oil lamp, I contemplated my feeling and then composed the following poem:

> For three years I stayed here beyond the seas,
> Half the time groping in London fog.
> The roaring of people mixed with the boom of the cars
> Stupefied me, robbed me of breath.
> Man's life keeps him in this predicament!
> I often wandered in the middle of the street.
> Suddenly in the long summer days I was free,
> Decided to go in search of peace.
> Long ago I heard the fame of the Lakes,
> This is the first glimpse of my old desire.
> Last night I came through wind and rain,
> Refreshment came into the depths of my heart.
> This morning I paid my visit to the lake and mountain,
> They smiled at me like relatives and friends.

Cunningly and rushingly they changed into a multitude
    of beautiful forms,
I thought I was not meeting them in a dream.
Suddenly clouds poured in from all sides,
It was hard for me to see their real face,
I did not notice my clothes were soaked.
Heavy rain poured down like a torrent.
In the twinkling of an eye it was clear again,
Fresh green made lovely the trees before the lake.
Alas! how could I come here day after day,
Leisurely just to be here and stay?

Afterwards, three more visitors arrived to stay in the same farmhouse. From their appearance they seemed to have walked a long way, and from their clothes they might have been climbing. We did not go to bed immediately after supper, but we all sat together in the hall, lit by an oil lamp hanging from the middle of the ceiling. The others were all talking and laughing together, but I did not dare to interrupt them to ask questions or break into their conversation, so I kept silent in an unobserved corner. I must say I felt a trifle awkward, for I might now appear to be overhearing their talk, and yet it was too early for bed, and it was both dark and wet out-of-doors. During a lull in the conversation, remembering that I must find out what I was to do in the morning, I took courage and addressed one of the gentlemen in some such words as these:

'I know nothing about these lakes; I came here through recommendation. I spent the whole of to-day looking round Wastwater and found it very beautiful—so many changes in mists, rain and sun. Yet I can't help feeling there are some other parts of the district which would give me quite a different impression. I am really anxious to see more; could you give me some advice about to-morrow?'

My new acquaintance thought a moment, then began to question me:

'Are you a good walker and climber? Did you really come here for climbing? Have you nailed boots with you? And how about your shorts and mackintosh? From here you can get to Buttermere, Keswick, Langdale, and some other places, but they need hard walking. Besides, it will be difficult for you to get back in the same day if you get as far as Keswick and places like that.' Eventually, after he had heard my standpoint, he advised me to go to Keswick or Windermere to join Coach Tours, and to see as much of the Lakes as possible in the short time. 'You will not see anything more here than you have seen to-day,' he told me. I nodded, and felt more puzzled in my mind than anybody there could have guessed, not knowing how to re-arrange my plans.

The whole house slept. I kept my candle-end burning; the flickering, dancing light seemed to keep time with my beating heart, as I lay down on my bed. I kept thinking to myself that I had no nailed boots and no outfit such as a 'hiker' wore, and how could I get to these places without them? And if I went to stay elsewhere for a night, what could I do with my baggage? Many problems tossed about in my mind—it may be out of proportion, through my tiredness and loneliness. I was especially afraid to move in case I should find no other vacant room in this busy holiday season.

August 2nd. Last night I slept a little, but in a disturbed way, and woke early in some depression. From my small window I could see the Great Gable deep in mist and heavy rain. I returned to bed until the maid knocked at my door for breakfast at 9.30. Over breakfast some of the visitors began discussing the weather; they were agreed that to be caught by rain was not so serious, but that to start out in it was far from pleasant. That was my own opinion also. I returned to my cramped bedroom; there was neither chair nor table, so I had to lie on my bed. From there I could look out of the window and watch many types of people walking through the rain to attend Sunday service in the tiny church at the foot of the mountain. It gave me inspiration for painting, for in painting I was always happy and could forget everything. Having no table, I squatted on the floor, got out my brushes, ink, ink-stone and paper, and converted the bed into a table. I painted the scene of the people going to church in the rain; the result was fairly pleasing, as you will see in Plate III. Next I painted one more sketch in recollection of my wanderings yesterday near a stone bridge with many pine trees behind it. Just at that moment the landlady came in to clean the room and found it in a strange disorder!

I went downstairs: two of the visitors had gone. I sat alone with the gentleman to whom I had talked last night. I ventured to ask him whether I might accompany him on his walk, and he replied: 'I am thinking of climbing Scafell if it clears up later; of course, you may come with me if you like to.' So we set out together. He was fully equipped for climbing, but I looked like nothing else but a London sightseer, with a small camera in my hand. By now the rain had stopped, but the peaks were still misty. Before we had gone far we found ourselves impeded by streams, and every place was terribly wet. My companion was worried about my thin shoes and socks, but though these were soaked through already, I really did not care at all. We came to the foot of the mountain and asked the footpath from some campers; I could guess from their looks of surprise that they doubted my power to climb that stiff peak in such everyday clothes. As soon as we struck the right path, we climbed on and on—I had no difficulty. Presently rain fell again, heavier and heavier—all the immediate surroundings were blotted out, nothing to be seen but a few stunted trees, the grass under our feet and occasionally a sheep. Among all the animals in this part of the country, sheep are the most plentiful. That is one of the things which struck me most in pondering the difference between England and my own country, because I have seldom seen sheep wandering among the hills in Central China, although in the Northern parts one meets them occasionally.

Presently my companion told me that we were now about a third of the way up. As a matter of fact, I had had no intention of making a serious climb when I started out, so I decided to part company, and turn back by myself at this point. I sat for a while on the brow of the mountain and gazed down on to Wastwater in the valley and the rain-cloaked mountains lying beside it. The splendid scene filled me with joy! Before the rain began I had not really noted the differences of colour in sky and mountains, but now I sat to contemplate the immensity of Nature covered by these masses of grey and white particles—behind them all there must be a vast assembly of forms, still and in motion, beyond expectation. In the very remote distance, as far as my eyes could reach, there was no visible joining point between the sky and the water of the lake; but the ruffled shining surface of the water with its reflection of clouds showed no break. I felt that I was sitting before a huge white polished wall, or, say, rather a vast grey canvas without edge waiting for something to be painted upon it. It was so, but there was besides a strong feeling of a movement of something on the canvas that could not be erased. The Screes were entirely invisible and only a faint and dim broken line of the range appeared in part at my left-hand side. After I had taken off my spectacles, I could count the white particles striking on my face; then suddenly I noticed a huge mass of clouds rolling forward on to me from the opposite side of the Screes. I can only describe the sight by the Chinese popular phrase, 'A dragon coming down from the Heavens.' My breath came with difficulty, my eyes were dazzled and my body grew stiff in amazement at the startling power of this mighty manifestation of Nature. I felt myself as a great giant at that time, for I could see no other living creature, even the tiny sheep eating grass a few yards below my feet was hidden. In

Chinese legends and novels we often read of an immortal being acknowledged by a dragon sent down by order of Heaven, and how he rode upon it to visit every part of the world. The setting was fit; might I not be the immortal at this time? Such was my fancy! Gradually the clouds and mists began to sweep away from Middle Fell towards Yewbarrow, and finally to Kirkfell, till the whole valley was radiant. I was sitting among the fresh green again and could still hear the sound of the rain dropping on the leaves. The colour of the Screes became brilliant purple against the sunshine in contrast with the dark green peak and black rocks of some part of Middle Fell on the other side of the lake. Within a few minutes the scene was transformed into something almost more wonderful than one could imagine. This experience added one more unfamiliar sensation to my mind; I had never seen anything to resemble it among our mountains and rivers. For the instant I realised myself and my whole existence as a human being to be an infinitesimal part of this mighty Nature. Scientists try to invent methods of concocting good colours; artists try to imitate all sorts of colours revealed in the natural scene, and poets try to use colourful words for depicting it; but, after all, methods, imitations and words are all strictly limited and soon exhausted, and no one can attain to an adequate expression of Nature!

I walked down slowly and thought over the scene I had just witnessed and a poem gradually composed itself, depicting only the first part of it:

> The mountain is lofty and rugged,
> I breast it smilingly—the white clouds clasped beneath my arm,
> And Heaven looks down with envy on my peaceful wandering.
> How rapidly the skies drop their wild torrents!
> I lie upon a rock in leisure and thought,
> Don't even know my clothes are wet.

I stood by the side of the lake for a little while and returned before six o'clock. Not very long after my companion returned also. He told me that he had to abandon the attempt; he said he would make another attempt to climb Scafell the following day. He had been four times in the Lake District and had made this visit specially for this purpose. My sole worry had nothing to do with climbing, but what I was to do next—whether to stay in Wastwater, go to Keswick, or even return to London. This evening there were four more visitors in the house; after supper they invited me to join them in a game of cards. Although I told them I could not play, they insisted on teaching me. Alas! I quickly lost points and was 'out.' And so to bed; to-night I had a new candle, by whose help I was able to refresh my memory of the day's impressions.

Plate II is a drawing of two peaks along Middle Fell in the mist and drizzling rain. The clear-cut outline of the mist coming out from the gap has been discussed by some of my friends, who could not believe such an appearance could be true. But such was what I saw with my own eyes.

Plate IV is a drawing of the tail part of the Screes after rain, from which the sound of great volumes of water running down could still be heard.

湖匪畫記

iii
Derwentwater

August 3rd. When I woke this morning I made up my mind to go to Keswick. I thought I might stay for the night if I could possibly find a place to sleep, and go back to Wastwater the next day. In the last resort, I thought I could ask a policeman to put me up somewhere, even the police station! The only worry in my mind was the trouble of dealing with my two small suitcases.

I breakfasted at eight; my friend was already up also, for he was off to Scafell once more! It was not a bright day, but for the time being there was no rain. He collected his kit and we set out of the house together; he told me that this time he would climb from the other side, near Sty Head, so we could walk a part of the way together. He assured me that I should have no difficulty in finding someplace to put up for the night, and that I might also find a motor tour that would bring me back to Wastwater.

Our ways parted, and I took a path that rose above his. After a while I looked downwards to pick him out; I could see a tiny yellow-brown spot moving along beside the stream; I was sure he had not struck his path yet. Then the mist spread across the valley from Lingmell to Great Gable; I was just in the middle and was caught by torrential rain. I walked on steadily and walked out of it eventually. I sat for a while on a rock and saw nobody. It was early enough.

I looked backwards occasionally while I was walking and could see Wastwater very small, like a mirror hanging in the far distance with a green background, and as the thick mists began to cover all the mountains and ground, the lake changed its form and became like the moon on a cloudy evening. My mind was quieter now than it had been at all, because I felt myself facing another world where there was no fear and no worry, although there might be minor discomforts, such as changeable weather. But I really believe it is just this changeableness of Nature that distracts so many poets, painters and travellers. They write, they paint, they discuss some special aspects of a scene, but for all their effort the great wholeness of Nature remains untouched. They admire it, they appreciate it, and they rejoice at it. But I do not think those words— admiration, appreciation, and rejoicing—are able to express one's immediate sensuous relation to it. I think one simply feels that it is beautiful if one is capable of direct sensation! A Chinese phrase, 'ling-lueh' is a good one for expressing one's reaction if one is trying to analyse one's enjoyment of Nature. 'ling' means 'to perceive or to receive an impression' and 'lueh' means 'a sketch.' These two words put together have the arbitrary meaning 'to accept into the understanding,' though it is difficult for me to find an exact English equivalent. When we are looking at scenery we say we want to 'ling-lueh' the beauty of it. I thought I was able to 'ling-lueh' the beauty of Wastwater at that time.

As I stood up to start walking again, on the right-hand side I found myself facing all kinds of different shaped rocks along the ridge of Scafell—some of them were clear in outline, some lay in a thin layer of mist, like the body of Venus covered with drapery, and the forms of some could only be guessed at. They seemed alive and mobile in accordance with the movement of the mist. How beautiful it was! I walked again, and looked admiringly at the brilliant green grass; but before I knew, I found my feet so deeply sunk in mud that I could hardly draw them out. I washed my feet and shoes in the stream, and after that walked along the bed of the stream. I made a poem to describe this moment as follows:

Strange crags ponderous and dignified,
Like lion, tiger and elephant.
Proud of strength in my body and limbs,
I struggle on energetically.
The way is loud with drizzling sound, but nobody have
    I met,
Stream-water tumbles clamouring over the path.

After a while I passed a small tarn beside the path; it may have been 'Sty Head Tarn' or 'Sprinking Tarn' according to the map; when I walked up to a signpost to find the name I came upon two cyclists—they were having great trouble in pushing their machines over the steep Pass, and I very soon left them behind. It was then bright and sunny, and many people were coming over the Pass from the other side. I met many looks of surprise; I suppose they did not often see a Chinese person in those parts.

As I neared the end of the Pass a new expectation came into my mind. I had been walking for more than three hours and all that time had not seen a single tree on my way, but only green grass, tiny flowing streams and undulating hill ranges; the rocky part of Scafell was far away in the distance from my present road. Just at that moment I saw scores of tree-tops down below the Pass, which led me to imagine I was about to come upon a wonderful scene. As I walked on downwards the slope was rather steep and the sound of a waterfall could be clearly heard. There were about twenty people, ladies, elderly gentlemen and children among them, coming towards me in the opposite direction. Some carried sticks to help them along, some appeared very cheerful with the sunshine reflecting on their faces, and some were pointing out positions as they reached the top of the slope. We glanced at each other and exchanged a 'Good morning.' I reached the end of the Pass, walked through a stone gate and found myself a stone wall to lean on, facing the waterfall which came curvetting and cascading down in all possible angles—it was probably Taylorgill Force. This was the second waterfall I saw since I came to England. Although for size and grandeur this could not be compared with Swallowfall which I saw in North Wales two years ago, yet it gave me more pleasure, for I was able to 'ling-lueh' its beauty as long as I wished, instead of being called away to join the coach after a few minutes, as happened at Swallowfall. The trees growing on both sides of the big channel of crags seemed like page boys that held the royal silver robes of the Force as it majestically ascended in some ceremony at Westminster. But this Force was continuously pouring, and I had to admire the trees for never growing tired of holding robes year after year. Just in front of my feet the stream received the waters of the Force and passed on to its boundless destination unknown to me. At my back was an elm tree, which seemed like someone holding a giant umbrella to protect me, like an Eastern monarch. But no, I could never be a king of that kind! I might rather be like an ancient Chinese general sitting before his tent with an attendant to hold a huge standard by his side; the roaring of the waterfall might well represent the sound of cavalry approaching before my eyes. It would be a proud feeling! Oh, but my sensation was not quite like that either. There was a painting in the Chinese Exhibition last year, *Gazing at the Moon*, by Ma Yuan; I felt I was the man in that picture, but without attendants, and gazing at a waterfall instead of a moon, peacefully and meditatively. How rare an experience!

After a long time my tranquil mind was stirred to the consciousness of cars upon the main road; I started to walk again. About 12.15, I arrived at Seatoller, and from there caught a 'bus to Keswick. On the road I felt in quite a different mood from that of my former journey from Seascale Station to Wasdale Head. It was raining now, too, but the sound I heard was not only the running streams and pines blown by the wind, but mainly the noisy clatter of the 'bus. I looked through the window and seemed to see the mountains growing one after the other in front of the 'bus and chasing each other at great speed. My mind followed the shapes of the successive ranges, in full harmony with them. As the 'bus turned at corners they seemed to run a little slower, and I could receive the impression of those richly green mountains in rain, as shown in Plate V.

On arriving, I made haste to find an English friend of mine, whom I knew to be staying there, but was unable to locate the address. However, I was fortunate enough to find a vacant room in a boarding-house that was advertising 'Bed and Breakfast' in the parlour window. Next I discovered to my pleasure that there would be a motor-tour visiting five lakes, including Wastwater, so that I should be able to collect my baggage tomorrow.

The first thing that took my attention was the town hall, which was designed on entirely different lines from all other buildings of that type I have seen in England. Unfortunately I have very little taste for drawing buildings, although it was pretty in its way. Here I found many people gathered in groups or walking about in the tiny, narrow streets, buying postcards or photographs of beauty spots. Because the town was so small and the streets so tiny and short, I really felt oppressed with the problem of over-population, a problem which some politicians made an excuse for war. Actually it cannot be so serious as to call for such drastic remedies! Keswick advertised itself as a good place for holiday-makers, by the numbers of picture shops, hotels and restaurants in every street. After I had sent a telegram to a friend of mine who was just then staying at Cheltenham, I walked back to my new lodging.

I was full of joy, especially when, following some other people to the lake side, I found Derwentwater, at a glance so different from Wastwater. There were all sorts of people moving about at the landing-stage, boatmen shouting for custom, and white swans floating round in a circle near the island; I was reminded instantly of the Chinese Westlake in Hangchow. It set my imagination working as to whether it had a sort of dyke and bridges to join the island to the other side, where the people could walk and watch the boating as it passed through, and what lay beyond the mountains on both sides of the lake. The answers to these queries could only be discovered after a few days' stay. I roused myself from musing and determined to join a motor-boat tour for a 'bird's-eye view' of the whole lake. The boat was crowded—all I could find was a seat outside the engine room. Though it was fine when the boat sailed, before long mist covered all the mountains, ranging from a thin purple-bluish layer to a thick grey and black one, and the rain came on suddenly heavier and heavier. The boat rocked on the lake, the motor engine pitting itself against the wind produced a very discomforting sound, together with the row of the passengers. Most of them crouched under their coats and mackintoshes, but I only took off my spectacles, and enjoyed looking at the great grey and then white mass of powerful Nature. It began to clear up afterwards when the boat turned round to the other side of the lake, and we returned to the same landing-place. All the time my feelings were occupied in comparing the differences of Wastwater and Derwentwater. The former was somewhat like a beautiful woman bathing without much clothing on her body; and sometimes she dived into the great white mass of cloudy Nature, which made her invisible or left only a vague image. Though she was mysterious, yet she had great dignity and strongly held to her own conception of morality. But Derwentwater was like a fully dressed lady in green-and-blue gown with all sorts of jewels and ornaments, who sometimes sat behind a gauze curtain which, though it might cover her face and obscure it a little, left her charm still visible. Of course, I could not judge the latter completely from a first glance, but I was fairly sure that she had more reasons to attract people to her than her harsher sister. And I fancy most people would agree with me.

Lucky in one more respect that evening, on my way back to my lodging I met the friend, Mrs Everett, whom I had hoped to find, and her friend with her. As she had sent me a card to arrange a picnic at Lodore Hotel, a place she thought I could easily reach from Wastwater, she was surprised to see me here by the side of Derwent. They were both very kind to me and invited me to dine with them; afterwards we had an interesting discussion on sketching. After dinner they showed me some of their water-colour sketches, and I promised to show mine as soon as I could bring my case along from Wastwater. My mind was full of this plan, and I had no other thought for the next morning.

August 4th. Today's experiences have nothing to do with Derwentwater. I thought it best to keep the record of events in order as they happened to me. I had a sound sleep last night and woke up early to contemplate the distant view of mountains through the window. I was very delighted to have a letter from the friend in Cheltenham. After breakfast I walked to the lake side and stood at the edge of Friar's Crag. There were very few people to be seen on the way. A morning mist overspread the surface of the mountains as it shifted away. I tried to describe this scene in one of my poems:

> Ringing the Lake are all blue mountains
> Compete for the honour of being its king.
> In and out between the mist and cloud,
> Cunningly they form, reform, and pass from view
> My heart rejoices in the morning,
> As leaning on a pine I catch the echo of a distant song.

The motor tour started at 10.30, and there were seven of us in the party. It was a disappointing excursion—I knew it would be so beforehand—for the car drove too fast and the driver was a man without taste, shouting the names of lakes and mountains, pointing out the properties of famous noblemen, etc., without giving us any opportunity of enjoying the actual scenery. Bassenthwaite Lake passed without our knowing what it looked like. I almost felt like bandaging up my eyes and ears, the process was so irritating! It was raining heavily. He tried to point out to us the Scottish hills, but there was no trace of them through the mist. Next he came to the subject of Germans bombing a particular spot during the Great War, and the word 'war' made my heart sick; why must men talk about such things in the midst of beautiful scenery? It was not for historical research that we were making this tour! Alas! the rest of my fellow passengers seemed to show interest in this information, judging from their faces. I thought the driver must have been trained to talk in this way to suit his clients.

At Whitehaven we got out of the car to stretch our legs; I strolled down to the seaside and took two photographs. I saw a score of people fishing on the beach and wondered to myself how they enjoyed the scene and the occupation.

We had lunch not far from there in an hotel near Gosforth, where I had walked three days ago. We looked into Gosforth Church, and the driver pointed out a specially fine cross with exquisite carving, apparently dating from a very early period. I was surprised indeed to see a bronze bell made in China for a temple in Ch'ing dynasty; I wondered greatly how it came to be there. Then we were driving along roads very familiar to me already. On the way to Wasdale Head the driver tried to remark cleverly: 'This place is so wild and lonely that, though you think you might like to build a house here and live for the rest of your life, the day would come quickly when you feared to be murdered!' The rest of the party laughed amiably at his remark, but I kept silent and again felt sickened—after all, why should people be thinking of murders and horrors?

After I had collected my suitcases, we were driven to Coldfell, Loweswater, and Crummockwater, etc, but I could only hear the names—some not familiar to my ears at all—and could not distinguish the places from each other. About 4.30 in the afternoon we reached a place called Scalehill Hotel, and there I had a leisurely look at the surroundings while the party went into the hotel for tea. It was a very fine afternoon. The sunshine on the trees and grasses brought out their greenness after the rain. I imagined that road must be a popular way for visitors passing through, but fortunately there were not many people at that time. I walked down from the hill and reached an invisible bridge underneath the road. The lake was hidden from me by a clump of pine trees which, I thought, were typical in lakeland, straight and ranged in the order of a troop of soldiers. At some distance to both sides of these pines there were no other trees at all. I could walk to the lake side easily, but I preferred to stand there and imagine the appearance of Crummockwater. Below the pines, I could see the distant hills, a range very similar indeed to some part of my native mountains. A stream emerged from the lake and ran under my feet smoothly with sometimes small wrinkles on its surface where the breeze caught it. I was intoxicated by the tranquil environment: not a sound could be heard except the running stream. I suddenly remembered there was a well-known Chinese poet who thought the sounds of thunder and running water the two most beautiful kinds of music that existed. He declared that the former could only be heard occasionally and that it was weird, strange and mysterious, and had better be listened to in a mood of anger, heroism, or adventure. But there were many types of sound for the latter—that of water falling, of flowing into the distance, of swirling or billowing, of breaking on rocks, of lakes, of rivers, of streams, and so on; one could choose to listen to any of these, and one's mood might be altered in accordance with it. There the sound of the small running stream I heard might have been one of his types—it was like a pair of lovers whispering and laughing under the trees with lowered voices; their words were not audible, but had they been the happy chatterers would never have cared.

Suddenly I found the driver standing by my side and telling me we had to go. I was relieved to get back to Keswick, and I spent a happy evening showing my sketches to my friends of last night and having a long talk about the different techniques of painting.

August 5th. I woke up to find a brilliant morning. I had a plan in mind to walk all round the edge of Derwentwater, because I should have liked to paint a long roll, showing the scenery of the whole lake. I was told the circumference was about eleven miles, so I had to make an early breakfast. I had a feeling for painting that morning, and I knew I should be able to observe the natural scenes with more than usually acute observation. I remembered, last night, talking to Mrs Everett about the power of memorising objects; she had confessed to fallibility in this respect and always preferred to paint with her eye on the scenery. But as for myself, trained in the Chinese tradition, it is no hardship to carry the shape of the mountain-contour in my mind's eye, and even the general colour scale. Light and colour in Nature shift with such subtle rapidity that I defy any artist to catch them exactly with his brush at any given stretch of time!

After I had reached the lake side, I stood by the railings and looked carefully towards the foot. Suddenly I found a horse ambling up to me and nuzzling its nose into my hand, as if looking for something to eat. I felt distressed, for I loved horses, but had no food for it at that moment. It was early and very few people were about yet. Presently it cantered away down the field neighing, and I sighed in response. There were four or five other horses scattered about the field—one had its head down munching grass, one was standing vacantly, and two or three more were gambolling together. When my new acquaintance trotted up to them he brought out a long whinny, which seemed to report that 'this foreign gentleman would not give him anything to eat,' but fortunately they kept their usual silence. The sunshine gleamed on patches of their backs and made a most beautiful splash of reddish brown colour among the bright greens—I am always amazed how Nature adjusts colours together in such harmony!

Next I came to the boats' landing stage; looking across to the other side as far as I could see, the mountain ranges stood out clearly against the blue sky and even the beams of the sunlight could be separately counted. The morning smoke was steadily puffing up from the chimney of some house hidden in the mass of trees and only a roof might be hazily discerned through the mist. I have always loved this sort of morning mist among trees. I suddenly thought there might be a giant still lying down there after his sleep, on a huge green bed made of leaves and tree-tops and steadily blowing cigarette smoke from his mouth! A fantastic notion! When I looked downwards to the surface of the water, I could pick out the shapes of two swans peacefully swimming and apparently gliding towards me with some pleasure. The placidity of my own mind at that moment fell in well with their motion, and I seemed in some way to be sharing it with them. But before long, more and more people began to approach the same spot and the boatmen to advertise the prices and times of motor-tours round the lake. I decided to move on.

I followed a footpath until I came to the road for Friar's Crag. There I found a little wooden gate, by which stood an elderly man and a young boy, whom I judged to be his son. They were selling hand-coloured postcards. The father was applying the colour, while the son praised their merits and explained the locations. I bought a couple. I passed through the gate and walked up towards the John Ruskin Monument and looked at the Catbell range above some tree-tops with considerable interest. To me it had the appearance of a camel's back with its one hump, and of the long head and neck lowered into the water to drink. I remembered the outline carefully, and then walked on and stood at the head of the Crag for some long time: the morning mists lying between the distant mountain ranges left their outlines indistinct, and the evasive, thin, fresh, gentle nature of the mists themselves gave a pleasant sensation to the mind. Suddenly I noticed a moving speck upon the lake water a long way away; it looked to me like an insect dancing upon the surface of a small pool; eventually it revealed itself to me as a rowing boat containing a young man and girl; I imagined they must be very happy on such a morning! I composed a poem about it:

Peacefully the small boat rocks upon the water,
While the white clouds scud across the blue,
My eyes newly delighted in the lovely scene,
As standing by a sheltering pine, I gazed into the distant
    hills.

Then I walked on alone again, taking the left footpath from the Monument, leading past Barrow Bay. There were many cows chewing grass on the flat meadowland. One of them seemed to sense a stranger, and ambled up to me with a sort of welcoming sound, or so I imagined: I stroked her hide. We seemed to have made friends. Presently some other people came along the same path and reminded me I should move on. My way led then through woods, so that I could no longer see the mountains. The path was very wet. I took the opportunity of eating my sandwich.

Before long I came upon a small wooden bridge, with a tiny stream running beneath it; I lingered there for a while, and then found myself at the end of the path; there seemed

三年留海外半屬倫敦霧人
聲雜車聲苦悶悶夢往生
活太覊人躑躅衔中路長
夏忽忽浮間立意尋出趣之
耳湖畔名風頗才一顧昨夜風
雨來清新入肺腑見起謁潮
山舎笑九親故紛紛騁奇觀
應化夢中遇俊乐宮四發真
西雜相瞪不覺濕衣衫大
雨傾多注轉眼又收晴像貌
湖哥樹安浮吕東萬事关
間住 初墨氏斯特湖

Plate I — Morning Mist on Wastwater
Translation of the poem is on pages 17–18

奇石森磷之以
狐兒兒象自負
腰脚健鼓勇爭
前往瀯々不逢
人一路清泉響
赴德韻特湖逢中

Plate II — Mist on rocky hills opposite the Screes, Wastwater
Translation of the poem is on page 27

一山高巋發笑揮
白雲入清遊遭天
忌狂雨來何急倚
石自悠然不知衣
袂濕
癸亥高山中途遇雨 啞

Plate III — Going to church in the rain, Wasdale Head
Translation of the poem is on page 22

樸被住湖中避
囂謝群眾一絲
夜氣清于平泉
聲遠待月々不來
吾去溫吾夢

韻湖夢待月 唖

Plate IV — Fine afternoon, Wastwater
Translation of the poem is on page 48

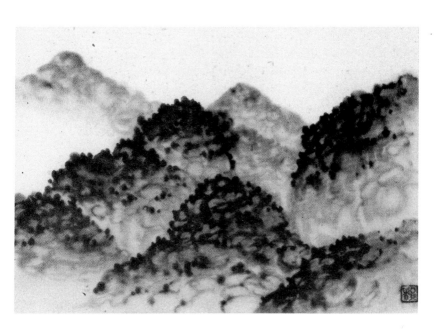

一葉中流開湖開石雲飛去
又飛還眼前好景新如故
獨倚蒼松看遠山
　右立齊執乎斯磯項
湖與詩人同不朽詩回湖
有十分清我來偏遇蕭蕭
雨滴碎秋心是此聲
　右中詩邁舲途斯唯
　　　　　　　　　[印]

Plate V — Mountains in rain looking through the window of a bus from Seatoller to Keswick

Translations of these poems are on pages 36 and 66 respectively

開闔景萬千我
欲窮其變煙外
好青山何為舊
所戀水鳥不避人
上下鳴春々
立德韻結湖畔 哐

Plate VI — View opposite the Scalehill Hotel
Translation of the poem is on page 50

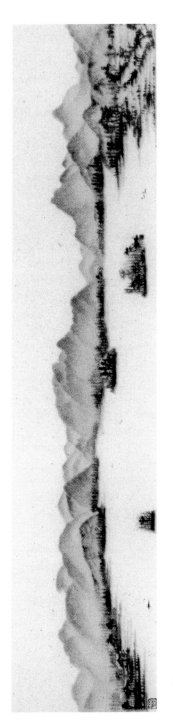

湖光勢雄壯不亞衡湘

湖山爭勝絕物我不干竿

探幽臺上寒煙可比岳陽樓

Plate VII — The charm and gentleness of
Derwentwater

Translation of the poem is on page 31

唯美在自然韻

湖我所愛四圍綠

無聲山生領清籟

我有會心寰宇在

湖山外

獨步德韻特湖畔呈

Plate VIII — Cows in Derwentwater
Translation of the poem is on page 41

山光淺映夕陽紅小立
湖邊與鷺濛蘆葦沼鱼
大自主獨来狐往碧波中
右八德在湖畔孔立

青山為枕沙為茵一眠湖
灘亦可人我心已在自然
外任汝白鷗来往頻
右怀八德在湖濱上

Plate IX — Horse in Buttermere
Translation of these poems are on pages 55 and 56 respectively

暑興曉霧弄縠

絞一白湖山不可

分花底清香葉

上雨祇容瞹生

靜中聞 呲

雨中

Plate X — Pine in Crummockwater
Translation of the poem is on page 49

新樣越山斜射陽約的
新港漾後飛汲清海一片
美人面見湖色沒
連絡灣折名放林曉夫臍
公湖嶺斯圖

Plate XI — Windermere
Translation of the poem is on page 69

Plate XII — Grasmere and its island in rain

to be no other leading round the lake side. A farmer, thinking to help me, pointed the way to the tarred main road. I had to thank him for his kindness, but I had no inclination to follow that fine, straight, but noisy motor-road. There was no more chance for peaceful contemplation, so I put my best foot forward until I reached the place called Barrowdale House, even though there was a stream bubbling a good part of the way. It was very fine there. I leaned on a stone wall and gazed back at Gowder Crag for a little while, which was formed entirely of aqueous rocks and reminded me of Li Cheng's typical style of painting in the Sung dynasty (AD 960–1279). He had a way of painting limestone rocks with a square brush-stroke, just as one sees this kind of formation in Nature.

The day seemed very long; the continual sunshine made it pass slowly. Presently I came to a small place called Grange, which lay at the head of the lake. There was a stone bridge there built rather like one which stood at the foot of my native mountain in China; even the surroundings had a familiar air, with the exception of the buildings and the cars parked at the side of the road. I remembered so well how I had played by that bridge as a child, with the children of my neighbours; how we had paddled in the stream to search for small crabs under the stones, because the water at that place was clear, shallow and not too wide. It was a great joy to move stones in the water, and we were so absorbed in our pleasure that we often forgot to go back home at mealtime. To our good fortune, few people interfered with us; sometimes our parents sent servants to us with food. At this moment I kept gazing down into the bottom of the stream, but there was nothing to be seen. The more I looked round the more the difference pressed itself upon me; and yet it was a very beautiful spot, with the lake on one side and mountains on the other. I wished strongly that I could have come here in the very early morning before people began to stir. Turning my head, I suddenly became aware of groups of people lying here and there on the grass, laughing and talking; the bright red and yellow colours of the ladies' clothes forced upon me even more inevitably that I was among strangers. Involuntarily I felt different and I was a stranger among them myself, and crossing over the bridge, began to move to the west side of the lake. Keeping on my way, I was obliged to follow the motor-road, for I could find no footpath. Sometimes I could see the east side of the lake very clearly; sometimes the twining of the road took it out of my sight. I could not actually see the Lodore Falls on the opposite side, but I could pick out clearly where they lay. At one point I was startled out of my musing by a red squirrel who leapt across the branch of a tree just in front of me, with brightly shining eyes. I had never seen a red squirrel before, so I looked at it with particular care. It was very interesting to watch, as it bounded about up and down the tree, with its startled eyes glancing here and there; suddenly it darted over the road where the sand and rock were yellowish in colour, so I lost all trace of it.

As I was nearing Keswick again I came across a man painting, with a lady knitting by his side. I imagined they must be husband and wife, and that they must have a contented family life! The journey home was very tiring, partly because I had already walked a long time, and partly because of the noisy cars running along the wide paved road. Very few people were walking on the road besides me; I thought that the car drivers might probably find me a nuisance and might say, contemptuously, 'Oh, only a poor Chinese!' I took a rest on a seat, perched on a high cliff by the lake side and saw distant Skiddaw as if she were a noble lady of Elizabethan times sitting there with her robes and draperies widely spread around her of purplish and brown colour, and shining in the reflection of the setting sun. It was rather a contrast among all the greens of Derwentwater, but so prominent to the eye that one might imagine the lady was leading all her maidens in green and blue to conduct a performance on the stage of

Nature. She was dignified and noble without any motion of her head from whatever angle you contemplated her. The more you looked, the more charming you found her. She sat a little apart from the other mountains. You could study her more effectively from a distance, and I could not understand why the so-called Nature-lovers sneered at it, termed it merely a promenade and even refused to admire its steep grassy slopes and 'double front' as I read in books. I was very lucky to have seen it in clear and fine weather.

I reached home about a quarter-past-eight; it had been a long walk and I was really tired out. Many thoughts were coursing in my mind, especially comparisons of this scenery with my native land. Some radical differences were there to be sure, but I could not find out what they were at that moment. Those friends—the mountains and waters of China—might have stared at me unrecognisingly now, because I wore European clothes! After this day I had the whole panorama of Derwentwater in my mind; it returned over and over again in my thoughts during the night and I was able to scan all her charms from many a different angle.

August 6th. As I was tired out after yesterday's ramble, I got up rather late this morning. Out of doors it was raining, and I could not see the scenery very clearly. I felt somewhat depressed, for I was awaiting a letter that did not come. I breakfasted at half-past nine; the newspaper lay beside my plate, but I had no courage to look at it, for I could imagine how the front page would be scored with the words 'War' and 'Peace' and especially with the state of Spain. I was no partisan of either side in the Spanish Civil War, and I could not understand why human beings should prey upon each other like the beasts. Is war an instinctive passion in man? But in Spain the women were joining as well! Does war stand for a sign of the progress of civilization? I doubt this, for I can see no 'progress' in the essentials of modern war from that of primitive times. I can understand that a lion will kill and eat rabbit or deer, but I cannot imagine a lion from Africa eating one from America, however hungry it might be! Again, I can understand that a large fish in the sea will try to catch other small fry for its food, but Heaven has given the small fish the power of quick movement, so that they can more easily escape the big fishes' mouths. Besides, if the big and the small were not living in the same patch of water, the unpleasant situation would never arise; I can imagine that small fish can live peacefully enough in a small pond! Primitive war among men was a question of the strong killing the weak, but numbers for slaughter were comparatively limited, and there was no cunningly-planned *collective destruction*. The problem of modern warfare is a different one; there is no pitting of personal strength between strong and weak, nor the hunger of big fish in search of small victims. Wherein lies the incentive for present-day war? It must be our eagerness to 'civilise' each other! Confucius believed that human nature was good in origin, and that the parents of the future man must experience profound difficulties in bringing him up to a life of happiness and virtue. But with the advent of war this valuable life may be dissipated in a single shot or a single whiff of the gas-bomb. I do not think Christ or Buddha would have liked human beings to value each other so little! And you Religious Leaders of the world! Your followers appear devout and sincere when they kneel before your images, but they soon forget all your sayings when they wish to kill each other. Probably they twist these very sayings of yours to extenuate themselves! How are you going to rectify these things? Even the great artists are unproductive in these years; they are afraid to see their productions thrown upon the general bonfire. My feeling has carried me away in writing on this subject; my readers must pardon me!

Later I went out for a walk; it was raining still, but I even took pleasure in it, and there were very few people about. It is my opinion that a walk in the rain gives one the true opportunity of appreciating Nature. Mighty Nature hides herself in mystery and the changes one expects never come. Such scenery cannot be caught by the camera, and to paint it is hard. It is a beauty which does not immediately spring ready-made to the imagination. One only feels it when one has the immediate experience. Too many people, unfortunately, sit within doors and enjoy their comforts, unaware of the loveliness outside.

As I came to Friar's Crag and sat there for some time contemplating the scene, the distant mountains which I remembered to have seen yesterday were invisible, except for a vague hint of outline. The rain fell in sharp steady lines as if a Chinese screen made of bamboo were hanging in front of my eyes. It was a joy to sit there quite alone. Presently the rain stopped, but the shape of the mountains was still a puzzle, filled out with mist and cloud steadily moving among them. I know some prefer the stark, clear-cut outline of a mountain in sunshine, but for me I like the mysterious mist-clad shape. Is it a reflection of the perpetual antithesis we find in the world—science and philosophy, material and spiritual? Before long all the crests of the mountains began to peer out, a fresh green colour after the rain; this gave me a powerful impression of the beauty in this valley, and I composed a poem for that particular moment:

> The loveliness of Nature,
> And Derwentwater that I love,
> Folded in and cloaked with green,
> Sitting for a while to enjoy tranquillity,
> My questing mind goes forth and wanders far
> Beyond the lake and past the distant hills.

Then I looked at the Crag itself and liked particularly the arrangement of the pines and a few other trees that I could see from that elevation. I studied them carefully, with the intention of making them into a painting—the trees and the remote mountains at the head of the lake. I walked next to Barrow Bay, looking keenly at the changing colour of the opposite mountains. There were many people passing to and fro at this time as it was afternoon and without rain, but the wind was so strong that they shrank inside their coats as if it were winter time. I returned by seven o'clock, feeling uncomfortable and depressed. I asked myself whether it was merely exhaustion or some other reason, but no answer came before I slept.

August 7th. My morning newspaper with its fresh stories of atrocities from Spain was balanced by the pleasure of a letter from a friend, describing to me with great interest some new educational schemes. After breakfast I decided to pay a visit to Lodore Falls, for I had had no time to appreciate them the other day. And I might have another good look round the lake. I followed the same path as before, and stood on my familiar bridge, listening with pleasure to the sounds of water flowing; I wished I could have caught that other welcome sound—of pines blown by the wind, roaring dully like a distant sea. Without thinking I raised my eyes towards the rocky hills under High Stile and was immediately impressed again by their resemblance to those paintings of Li Cheng, the Sung dynasty artist. I looked at them thoroughly. It was very interesting examining those rocks; they were simply blocks of limestone, but grey in colour, with every fantastic shape imaginable. They were piled up upon a great mass of green grass as if Nature had specially planned a decorative scheme. There was some sound of water pouring from a height—I supposed a crack in the rocks, but could not find it anywhere.

Next I came to Barrow House, in front of which a line of stone steps stretched into the water; so clear it was that I could see the bottom. There were many small fish swimming about and clustering together in search of food. They looked happy and thoughtless, undisturbed by miserable reflections.

I felt sorry that so many people tried to catch these lively creatures with nets and lines. I myself have a curious love for fish; their vivid movement in the water attracts me, and I have the desire to make a speciality of fish painting! I was so happy in the sight of them at that moment that I began to hold a sort of imaginary conversation with them like a child, asking them whether they realised their good fortune, 'Do you feel the stifling war atmosphere above your heads?' I was compelled to ask, for my mind was obsessed with this subject just then. Water covers two-thirds of the world, but I doubted that its inhabitants had violent enmity among themselves, as did the inhabitants of the other third. 'Do you have the same feeling of differences in race, in nationality, in language, or in the terms 'Culture and Civilisation?'' Have you ever planned to group together for Collective Destruction or Collective Security?' I paused, naturally without an answer; the fish took no notice, but went on swimming as usual. I almost felt I should strip off my clothes and dive under the water to join them; then I should have no more public or private worries! There was once a Chinese philosopher, Chuang Tzu, who dreamed of becoming a butterfly; why should not I in my dream turn into a fish? Indeed it would be better for one to choose the fish's life, for a butterfly cannot live in storm, wet and cold. Just at that moment a fish about four or five inches long leapt out of the water. I looked at it in amazement and it scurried away with a flick of its tail. I wondered whether it had jumped up on purpose to attract my attention or to acknowledge my appreciation of their happiness. In the distance I saw two swans floating together on the water like a devoted couple; they seemed unafraid of men and came boldly up to a boatside. Their happiness was different from that of the fish! Then a motor-boat came along the lakeside, past the place where I stood. Its track ruffled the water, and after it had passed I saw both swans and fish had disappeared.

When I came to Lodore Hotel there was also a landing-stage made of timber. From its appearance it had been in disuse for a long time; there were flocks of water-birds gathered on it. At that moment I regretted having come that way, to drive them all off and break up their happiness. Other people came after me, and started to use the solid wooden pier for cooking their lunch on. I began to smell the odour of frying eggs and bacon, and with my own hunger roused I ate up my sandwiches.

I walked up the narrow path towards the Falls. As I listened to the roar of the tumbling water I easily imagined myself back in my native land, visiting the 'Yellow-Dragon Falls' of Lu Mountain. The entrances were almost identical, only as I reached the falls themselves I found these split into many branches, as there were rocks piled up in the middle of the channel; they were less powerful and severe than the 'Yellow-Dragon,' nor was there a pond at the base where the force could, so to speak, lie in reserve. I sat in the seat provided in front of the falls, and my mind simply wandered back to my home. I climbed higher up to where the volume of water was greater; I sat again on a large stone and thought over my past life, just as I had done once before, sitting by the waterfall of 'Heaven's Bridge' at Lu Mountain. Now everything in the past has passed already, and what is to come I cannot foresee. But Nature has never changed to me in moving from place to place; she differs only according to my changing states of mind. These falls, however different in appearance from those of my childhood, reproduced for me the same notes of natural music.

After this experience I walked over to Barrowdale Hotel and stood looking at the scenery from this point for a while. The rocks were beautifully arranged one upon another, and there were a few tiny houses built under a huge crag, which was dressed all in green and showed me again how similar Nature is everywhere. I do not know why people should always be pointing out the differences. I had tea in Mrs Pepper's garden, and that time there were many visitors. By my side at a long table a husband and wife sat and talked quietly. Presently three young ladies joined us; from their laughter and cheerful faces they seemed happy enough. Both parties had dogs with them, and before long they began to quarrel and disturb their owners; it surprised me and made me pay unwarranted attention to them.

Once again I walked along the west side of the lake and climbed up the hills under Catbell. Looking towards the distant mountains I found great delight in studying their varying shapes; I should have liked to linger, but a swarm of flying ants rose up all round me and drove me away. I caught a 'bus from Grange and arrived in Keswick by seven o'clock. Walking through the town I unexpectedly came upon one of my fellow countrymen. After a short talk we quickly became friends.

After my wanderings all day again I really felt I had the general structure of Derwentwater in my mind; sitting by the fire in the evening, I tried to recollect every detail. Artists can never hope to paint the real Nature, but only one aspect of Nature reflected in their own eyes. Our Chinese artist tries to paint the Nature in his mind, not the Nature in Nature, and so his pictures do not search for exact resemblance. Nevertheless, resemblance is inherent in his work, for it derives from genuine natural impressions. Suddenly that evening the complete picture of Derwentwater in mist came before my sight, and so I painted it as in Plate VII.

My heart began to beat insistently when I heard I should be able to see the moon that night! This was the beginning of my excitement, because I have a very deep love for her and I considered her all my life as my Soul's Companion. When I was still a little boy I used to sit in the garden of my home, perched on an ornamental rock, just to gaze at the moon. My mother died when I was only five years old, and my brother and sister were both much older than I, consequently I was frequently alone, and my temperament was, besides, well suited to moods of calm and tranquillity. There were many cousins living in the same house with us, with whom I could have played children's games had I wished, but I nearly always preferred to play by myself in the garden, especially after the evening meal.

The climate in China is rather different from that of England—colder in winter time, but dry; we can see the moon clearly at least fifteen nights in every month. When the Mid-Autumn Moon Festival came round, my excitement exceeded all bounds; I used to start waiting in the very early morning until it should be time for the moon to rise. As I grew up and began to read poetry, it was those poems about moonlight which delighted me most, and there are many of them among the works of our famous poets. I cannot say truthfully that I have never seen the moon in all the three years I spent in England, but seldom has she appeared to me without her face covered in clouds; I could never see her radiantly clear as in China, and so I am inclined to say that I have not seen my real friend the moon at all! But at that time I heard that I could see her indeed, and the landlord's description of her appearance in the lake made me think of her unceasingly.

I began to tell you before how I met a fellow countryman on my way home this evening; at first we had stared at each other strangely, not certain whether our judgment had been correct. When he saw my long black hair swept back from my forehead, he came over to speak to me. We naturally made friends on the spot, and it was an intense pleasure to have a real conversation with someone at last; since I had come to the Lakes I had lived almost dumbly. I told him that tonight there was to be a moon, and he leapt with joy; we arranged to meet after supper and row on Derwentwater. This was so familiar an occupation in China that we had a fixed phrase for it—'Boating under the moon'. When the friend and I had met at the landing-stage, we hired a boat and set out. My friend rowed first, but in the Chinese manner, which was the exact opposite of the Western way— forwards instead of backwards. The people on the lake side laughed derisively and shouted at him, and compelled us for our own peace to change the method. I myself had the impression that though the Western way may be speedier and more scientific, there is something poetic and appreciative in the Chinese one. If one rows facing the direction of the boat's progress, one can see what is approaching and can oneself avoid collisions. And so one's companion need not take such anxious care in controlling the rudder, but can abandon himself to enjoyment of the scenery. I also believed that the rower would derive more enjoyment from watching the scenery ahead rather than that which had just passed. However, as I said, to stop the shouting of the onlookers, we changed our style and I took on the oars.

It was not dark yet. I gazed on the mirror-like surface of the water and listened to the sound of the oars striking it steadily and rhythmically—Tsan, tze-tze-tze; tsan, tze-tze-tze... Once I felt I was ski-ing backwards on ice, and then I imagined the boat with its oars stretched out to both sides was like a dragonfly perching and skimming along the water surface. The mountains on both sides were apparently moving along as well, but showing their friendship to us as if they were coming out to welcome us one after the other. There were a few white spots on the water almost out of our sight that I believed were seagulls. It was very quiet, though there were some boats on the lake, but far away from ours. Then my friend took over the rowing and I sat in the stern to steer. I wrote a poem to express my feeling at that time:

> I sail through the heart of the lake plying my oar—
> On every side the leaping tops of the waves—
> Sit long till my body shivers with chilliness.

> All the water reflections are green shadows,
> And a mild breeze blows outside round the gunwale,
> Calmly awakens the seagulls from dreams.

Darkness had almost fallen, and we could not see the mountains clearly through the evening mist. The water presently became rather choppy, and we felt cold. We talked on many familiar topics and sang some of our native poems. We stayed there on the lake until every other boat had moored up for the night, but still there was no moon to be seen. I was more disappointed than my friend; he was quite prepared to go home by that time, but I was unwilling to abandon hope. I went over to Friar's Crag and sat there for a long time. The moon, my long-departed friend, did not come out to look at me at all. Imagine the depth of my sadness at that time! Another poem was composed as I went to bed:

> I came in haste to the lakeside,
> Thankful at escaping the press of the crowd.
> How pure is the night air...
> Feeding my ears with the rushing stream's music.
> I linger, waiting for the moon, but she never comes,
> Returning, I feed my burning love for her in dreams!

August 8th. Though I was disappointed in my vigil for the moon, yet I had happiness last night in dreaming. I saw the moon shining over Wang-Sung-Lin—a forest of pine perched on Lu Mountain. In the days when I lived near there, I often used to walk at night talking to the moon, and this was just such another experience—indeed, an even lovelier one, for in dreams we forget our insignificance and can face the moon herself like kings and queens, free from shyness.

I rose very late this morning. My landlady was surprised and said that she had knocked on my door twice to call me for breakfast. I made apologies to her, but I did not disclose that I had been meeting an old friend! After breakfast I felt disinclined to go out and somehow rather tired, preferring to sit indoors. There were all sorts of papers lying on a chair in the drawing-room, but I only turned them over carelessly. It was raining outside and there seemed to be no other sound except the raindrops on the leaves. Fortunately these lodgings faced a part of Derwentwater, but I could not see outside the window very clearly for the rain, so I moved a chair over and sat by the doorstep. There were some summer flowers of different colours blossoming in the front garden, among them were some brilliant roses growing close by my left side. I had no thought at that time, but only shifted my eyes from one object to another; sometimes towards the centre of a flower, sometimes to the pearly raindrops on the leaves, sometimes to the remote whiteness where the mist covered the distant hills, leaving no point visible where land joined water, and sometimes the lonely road. There was nobody in the house and at that particular moment I could not feel the existence of anyone anywhere. With contemplative mind, I sat for a long time. I could hardly believe that I should be able to keep such a tranquil state of mind during the busy season at the lake. I wrote another short poem also on that occasion:

> Rising at morning the mists hang in confusion,
> Unbroken whiteness links mountains and lake.
> There is clear scent deep in the flowers and rain upon
> the leaves;
> Sitting profoundly in calmness one may enjoy them.

Afterwards I went up to my little room and lay down in bed. No train of ideas came into my mind, but only an inclination to paint. Therefore I took out paper, ink and brushes, and made two or three studies of the mountains on both sides of the lake; I felt happy as I completed them, for they seemed to correspond with my imaginary plan better than usual.

The rain stopped about three o'clock in the afternoon. I went out for a walk and strolled slowly down to the lakeside, and stood for a while at the spot where the footpath ended, just opposite Hill-top. There were a score or so of seagulls driving against the wind, swiftly and fearlessly, crying rather like young children as they swooped and passed. I watched them fascinated. I had seen these birds over and over again on my journey to Europe flying round the ship; at this time I saw them among hills. I felt acutely the difference between this lake scene and my native landscape.

The air was clear and fresh just after the rain. It seemed to me that the universe had undergone a certain change, like a human heart newly washed by tears and so become calm and relaxed. There was still a sort of mist coming up from the surface of the water as if the whole lake had filled up with boiling liquid. Though several big bunches of clouds lay scattered here and there like woolly sheep lying upside-down on the sky opposite me, as far as my eye could reach there were patches of light picking out the land more clearly than ever before. A beam pierced one of the massive cloud-banks as I was watching and turned the edge of the cloud into silver and shone on the tops of the mountains. As the clouds moved onwards, the light changed and the brightness on the mountains shifted constantly. Suddenly I had a very peculiar feeling, hardly describable. I wanted to fly up into the cloud and to control the sun, like a film operator in the cinema! There was a very pleasant smell everywhere from the grass, trees and wild flowers. I imagined there must be a lot of people wandering about along the road to Friar's Crag, as it was a very popular part of the country, and I was glad to find myself out of the crush. I also wrote a poem about it:

> Widely open stretches the varied scene,
> And I would search its farthest distances.
> Beyond the mists the bluish mountains rise,
> Shadowy, like a long departed love.
> The seagulls, fearless, driving overhead,
> Cry childishly as they swoop and pass.

As soon as I reached the gate of my lodging, my friend came towards me from the opposite direction. He told me that he had been climbing Skiddaw all the day; there had been five of them altogether, but the weather had not been good. I said I would like to go up there as early as I could to see the sunrise; it would be a grand view, and probably very different from my experience of sunrise on board ship. Many of our country folk often go up a high mountain peak to watch it in China, and I myself had been three times to see the sun rising at Lotus-Peak in Lu Mountain. But it would not be so easy to arrange here as one never knew whether it would be sunny or raining on the top of a mountain in England! My friend and I had supper together and walked through the streets of Keswick town, but there was very little to see at night. At last we arranged to go to Buttermere the next day.

On my way home I thought over all my views of Derwentwater, and decided I had seen most of her variations, I wished I could stay there longer, as my affection for her was increasing every day. Her charm and her gentleness have made a lasting impression on my mind. And I had had a good opportunity of comparing every angle of Nature's life in this country with that of my own.

湖匜畫記

Buttermere and Crummockwater

August 9th. As soon as I reached the bus stop I could see my friend coming that way also, but it was still too early for the Seatoller 'bus. We took a short walk round the places nearby. My friend was surprised and a little shocked to see so many pieces of land enclosed and marked 'Private', protesting that in China we should never find the public forbidden a free enjoyment of scenery. I acquiesced, and admitted that it seemed money could buy even Nature!

And so we came to the bus, and drove off to our destination. On the way my friend showed me an extract from *The Times* discussing the Far Eastern question. I had no wish to read it, knowing beforehand the sort of comfortable generalisations on 'The Peace of Asia' it would be sure to contain: terms of deception for the public. For I could not believe in the possibility of widespread peace anywhere in the world these days, even though my own mind and environment were tranquil enough for the moment.

In half-an-hour's time we reached Seatoller and began walking along the Honister Pass, the lower part of which was a steep climb, though, busy with conversation, we did not notice it. On the left-hand side, going up, there was a narrow valley, where a twisting stream poured down swiftly as if there were scores of white snakes or eels chasing one after the other. Different kinds of trees stood along both sides to protect them. When we reached the upper part of the pass, which was less steep, we came upon a wide and rather neglected piece of grass land; there were no trees growing and there was nothing of interest to see except level mountain ranges. Just as we reached a rugged peak, facing Honister Crag, and I was on the point of taking a photograph, I discovered to my dismay that I had somewhere dropped my most precious notebook, containing almost all the notes of my lakeland excursions. I was seriously distressed, and began to trace back the way we had come. Eventually we found it lying in the wet grasses where many sheep had been straying. I was overjoyed, and so we resumed our path with new spirit.

There was a factory and a railway line to the side; I had been told that Honister rocks were famous for roofing slate. We walked down along the pass, which now began to descend rapidly, but this part was more cheerful than the ascent. The path undulated and a stream flowed on without ceasing; the banks on both sides were so high that one was made to feel like a pygmy walking down the middle.

About two in the afternoon we reached Buttermere. It was not one of the larger lakes, but set in a very lovely environment it seemed then a more than usually calm stretch of water. My eye was particularly caught by a distant mountain of rugged outline: it was actually on the border of Crummockwater, but from this point stood out clearly, as the weather was very fine. I looked back towards 'Robinson Head,' by the side of which I had been walking, and my eyes reached its fringe of tall, slender pines on the slopes. The mountains on the left-hand side and those a little farther away to the right made two crescents, which seemed to embrace the whole lake. As I walked back to the point where there were three trees, I stood there and had a whole view of the lake. Far away to the right there stood a group of pines and other trees with stones underneath, which seemed to me like a pier stretching out into the lake, but luckily there were no cargo boats around it. On the opposite side, I could see a stream running down along the slope of the hills, which, caught in the light, seemed just like a thin silver wire or a piece of string lying on a green blanket. It was extremely quiet on the water, even though two or three waterbirds made circles of wrinkles when they dipped down to catch fish. It was so calm—not a single breath of air even to set the leaves on the trees in vibration. I noticed two camps at the bottom of a hill, but even from them there was no sound rising.

Really it was a splendid day, with brilliant sunshine. My friend and I were drowsy, and after our mid-day sandwich we lay down to rest beside the water. The sky was clear and blue to-day, and there seemed no disturbing element. I just closed my eyes peacefully. The poem illustrates my mood:

> Blue mountain as pillow and sand for a blanket,
> It is pleasant to drowse upon the lake shore.
> My heart has already passed beyond Nature,
> Heedless of you, white seagulls, busily flying here and
> there.

My friend was fast asleep. I crouched on a rock and shared the rest of my meal with the fish. In watching them nibbling up some crumbs, I quite forgot my own existence until suddenly I heard my friend, who had woken at last, crying, 'Look out—you're being photographed!' I looked up to find an elderly gentleman standing on the other side of the fence with a camera. I smiled at him in acknowledgment and thanked him. Turning to my friend, I remarked that he had probably come into the picture as well and that his sleeping expression would be amusing to see! Those moments while I watched the swimming fish had somehow made a deep impression, so I made a poem about the scene:

> The mountain shines dully in the crimson sunset,
> I stand by the lake-side, profound thought stirs.
> Envy the swimming fish so free of care,
> Coming, going, solitary through the green waves.

About six o'clock we walked along to the point of land which linked Buttermere with Crummockwater. And there I had a view of Crummock—a wild and impressive lake so far as I could see, very different in character from what I could see of the rugged mountain at Buttermere. The shape of this mountain, its colour and its rocky surface, were vividly clear to me, but very changeable. There was a cushion of cloud moving about over the top of it like a sort of umbrella to protect it from rain, but in fact it really meant the rain would soon fall. Before long I saw spots on the water like pearls floating, few at first, but rapidly increasing in number, and my friend urged me to come away. As a matter of fact, I should not have minded standing in the rain, since the scene attracted me. As soon as we came to the hill-side, where we started from, I stood by a very beautifully shaped pine and looked at the lake again. The whole of it was not visible from that point, but it gave one some general impression and anticipation. I made this scene the subject of a painting (Plate X).

On the whole, I found Buttermere and Crummock very similar in appearance—they are both small, and surrounded with rather the same type of mountain—but the former struck me as being more particularly beautiful than the latter, which had wild beauty, but could not be compared with Wastwater. Unfortunately I could not see it fully, as it was partly covered by the evening mist.

It was pleasant to have had company to walk with after my long silent days in the Lakes. I was grateful, too, to my friend, who amused me with various humorous English anecdotes while there was nothing of interest on our road. I remembered a drawing in 'Punch' of a lady and a gentleman walking together, with words like these:

'She: 'What a magnificent sunset! How it lifts one's thoughts above the earth!'

He: 'Ah, that reminds me. You must speak to the landlady about our bacon in the morning. Tell her I like it streaky.''

So we laughed once more.

湖匪畫記

V

Windermere

ugust 10th. As we parted last night my friend asked me whether I should care to visit Windermere with him the next day. Neither of us would be able to make a long trip, and I had heard it was a large lake, whose whole appearance and charming character might not be caught in a hasty visit. However, we made the best of our circumstances and arranged to meet in the morning.

I rose rather early, excited at the prospect, and met my friend at the 'bus station about nine o'clock, but we were a long way ahead of time. I agreed to fill up the hour or two we still had in front of us with another visit to Lodore Falls, which he had not yet seen. On the way he showed me many photographs of mountain and river scenery round Kuei-Ling in the province of Kwangsi in South China, a district so beautiful that one could not really claim to have seen China had one never been there. On reaching the Falls, I sat again on my old wooden seat; it was still early and raining a little, so that I could enjoy an extraordinarily quiet time there without any disturbance. The sound of the water pounding and splashing on the rocks came to me clearly, together with the softer noises of rain on the leaves. After a while we took the bus back to town and started out for Windermere.

Passengers were few, to my surprise, for I had always believed Windermere to be one of the most important centres for tourists in all Lakeland. The rain outside poured down heavier and heavier as we went on, and soon, between the misted glass of the windows and the misty scenery outside, all view was quite shut out. I felt as chilled inside as if it were winter time. In my native city it is hot indeed at this time of the year, at least eighty degrees in the daytime. In those days we always longed for a shower of rain, but it never came. Presently my friend wiped one of the windows clear and told me that the Lake Thirlmere was in sight. I craned and peered, trying to get some impression of it, but could see little except a stone wall with a tongue of blue water beside it and part of a mountain foot at the opposite edge. It seemed to be a placid stretch of water, long and narrow, without any vagrant or striking features, but I could hardly judge fairly by a fleeting glance from the bus.

The bus went on and the rain fell again; I saw two more lakes, which I took from the map to be Grasmere and Rydalwater. They were small lakes and quickly passed. I assured my friend that since Grasmere was so near Windermere I must absolutely see it, for this was the home of the poet Wordsworth, through whom I had first had the desire to visit the Lakes.

We arrived at Windermere by lunch time and took our meal in a small restaurant. 'Alas!' I cried to my friend, 'we are back in London again!' For the streets were packed with people strolling about as if they were in Oxford Street or Piccadilly Circus, only with the difference that they walked all in one direction. We came to the lake side. I could not describe my sensations at that time; the people packed in rows looking at the scenery reminded me of a news film I had seen of the University Boat Race, while the ranks of cars parked by the waterside made me think of Derby Day. We walked along to the left and through a wicket gate, where the crowd was less; standing by the edge of the lake I had the momentary impression of being on the Yangtze River bank. For this lake was rather like a river from this viewpoint—so long that I could not possibly reach either end with my eyes. The mountains opposite, although partly obscured by mist, did not strike me as being very high, but they were luxuriantly vegetated with thick woods. The colours changed miraculously as the mists dispersed in one place and thickened in another, shifting almost imperceptibly. It amazed me where the red colour should come from that made such an incredible, unforgettable purplish layer over all the mountain face. On the extreme left I could catch a glimpse of the distant hills, comparatively low, and a uniform grey, relieved only by a patch of bright sky above them. On the very edge of the opposite side of the lake I could pick out two or three dark red or bright yellow spots, which kept disappearing from time to time. I imagined they must be ladies rowing in boats. The general scene was not unlike that part of the Yangtze River between Chenkiang and Nanking, though the atmosphere here was much damper than it ever appeared to be there, even in a rainy season, and besides differences in the form of boats and buildings, there was the noticeable difference in the water colour; this lake was a deep blue and the Yangtze, yellow.

We followed on to even quieter surroundings; the farthest part of the sky gave promise of a fine afternoon though the place where we stood was still heavy with gloom. I could not bear this heavy humidity! I tried to look constantly towards the brightness of the most distant hills, finding there the symbol of a clearer future in a time of hard work and depression.

The water grasses beside the lake edge delighted me as we walked on into the wilder parts; as the wind drove small waves to the shore the grasses seemed to bend in acknowledgment, and as the waves withdrew they raised their heads again proudly. They swayed and quivered with an air of dignity. I took out my notebook and made a few outlines of the mountains in case I should want to paint them later. Finally, my friend suggested we should take a steamer trip up the lake.

We reached the landing-stage at Bowness only to find a long queue of people waiting for the boat; it was at least a quarter of an hour before our turn came. In the meanwhile I watched these holiday-makers with great interest, hurrying, scurrying, everyone in haste and eagerness. I reminded myself that never could such a scene be found in China; in the busy West it seems that even merry-making has to be done in haste nowadays! When we started eventually, the steamer was packed with laughing, talkative people; but, nevertheless, the trip was more enjoyable in my point of view than my former excursion on Derwentwater, for the steamer itself had quieter engines and moved with some slowness and dignity over the water. The lake itself was even wider than I had imagined, and dotted with small islands. The name of the largest I overheard—Belle Isle—and it was long and beautifully wooded. Though it was by now late in the afternoon and rather dark, I could see some rowing boats darting in and out of sight. They gave a most decorative appearance to the lake. The mountains on either side passed from sight one after the other with an apparent movement both harmonious and rhythmic; this sight and the few seagulls following the steamer's wake made me oblivious to the laughter and noisy conversation of the other travellers. Presently we passed a rugged range very like a sea with towering waves rising one beyond the other as far as eye could reach, and the sunlight sparkling on one flank of them gave the appearance of snow. I could not help exclaiming aloud: 'How beautiful it is; I should like to stay here for ever!'

We disembarked at Waterhead soon after five o'clock. To my amazement I found a weeping willow standing on the shore. This tree is one of the most popular subjects in Chinese landscape painting, and this was the first time I had set eyes on it since I came to the Lakes. But still there was enough dissimilarity to remind me that I was far from home: the Chinese willow has a rugged twisted trunk and is rather low; this one was slender and tall with all its branches drooping, both decorative and graceful, very well fitted to the background of soft green hills. While my friend went to find out about the 'bus home I walked up towards the gate of Romney Hotel and looked down towards the lake with extreme pleasure. I think it is one of the most attractive scenes in all Nature to watch mists rising among hills just before nightfall. At this time the colours of the hills and trees, the movement of the clouds above the distant mountain ranges, and the late chirping of the birds, all filled me with indescribable sensations.

I was determined that I must see Grasmere, and so arranged to stay for the night at Ambleside, while my friend returned to Keswick. In the course of the evening I went to see an exhibition of Lake District watercolours which was being held there, but it was too late to get in. After taking supper in a very tiny cafe I went straight to bed. Before closing my eyes I found some lines of Wordsworth running through my brain:

> ... I overlooked the bed of Windermere,
> Like a vast river, stretching in the sun,
> With exultation, at my feet I saw
> Lake, islands, promontories, gleaming bays,
> A universe of Nature's fairest forms
> Proudly revealed with instantaneous burst,
> Magnificent, and beautiful and gay.

Oh, Windermere, Windermere, you will draw me back to you again soon!

湖匾畫記

Rydal Water and Grasmere

August 11th. When I woke I found it was late already and again pouring with rain. I started the day in complete idleness, eating my breakfast and turning over the morning papers, waiting for the possibility of the rain ceasing or at least becoming less. At last I set out on foot towards Rydal Water and Grasmere. On the way I met nothing remarkable; it was the same well-paved motor-road that I had already driven along. Following the map I came to what seemed no larger than a pond or tarn, but which could be in fact no other than Rydal Water! I could hardly believe my eyes! The hills round this piece of water were as beautiful as any to be found in the whole Lake District, but the lake itself was very small indeed, and greatly obscured by trees and wavy grasses growing in it. I wished there might have been large clumps of lotus or water-lily planted here, too, which would certainly have attracted visitors to linger for the sake of their charming blossoms.

I had to move on to Grasmere in case I should be short of time. It began pouring again. These torrents of heavy summer rain made me think of the autumn rainy season in China; we were grateful for its refreshment, because the end of the summer was always dry and hot, but now here one felt terribly wet and damp and heavy in every part of the body, even though there was lovely scenery before one's eyes. And it was not at all hot either. With my clothes soaking wet I came up to the side of Grasmere. Everything was covered by the mists and clouds and I had to take shelter under a tree. The drizzling sound of the rain on the tree leaves and the water sent my mind into channels other than the scene in front of me, so I wrote the following poem:

> The lake and the poet living together always,
> The poems and the lake water equally refreshing.
> At my coming, in every part the sad soughing of rain,
> This is the very sound to break the heart of Autumn.

From the translation of this poem, I cannot express the very deep feeling of my heart for the lake and the poet. I would have stayed on that spot for a very long time and buried myself in thought, if a sudden violent blast of wind had not roused me, reminding me that I was hungry and driving me into a small tea house for lunch. I now felt uncomfortable, with my clothes so terribly wet, and felt no inclination to go out again in the rain. I stayed on, hoping for a respite, until I was advised to go to Dove Cottage, where Wordsworth had lived for some years. It was an obvious subject of pilgrimage and visitors came from every part to this place in the little valley. Wordsworth had associations with many lakes in the district, but this was the one which attracted most people, probably because his grave and his cottage were there. I entered the cottage and felt that nearly every object there preserved some of the poet's personality. There are many of my countrymen who have the same keen interest as most Europeans in finding out which chair the poet had sat on and which bed he had slept in. I am afraid I am not that sort of person. I prefer to leave those things for the study of historians and archaeologists. What interested me most were the surroundings which stimulated the poet to compose his poems and convey his ingenious thoughts. I imagined his original environment at the time when he was composing must not be in the least like what we had now before us—so many people coming and going, so many hotels and cars. His feeling would have been very different had he lived in this sort of atmosphere. Anyway he has proved an unintentional philanthropist in finding so many jobs for people, and it was clever of him to have left so many things for the interest of visitors if they had little taste for scenery! I passed through the Wordsworth library and museum rather quickly, though I stayed for some time examining the original writing of the poet. Then I came to the church and saw the poet's grave, together with that of Hartley Coleridge. There was nothing remarkable about the stone which bore simply the few words of the poet's name. I remembered I had written a poem after my first visit to the Poets' Corner in Westminster Abbey, but at this moment I had no inspiration. There were many people in the churchyard, but fortunately the rain had stopped. Presently I thought about going to the lake side. On the way I began to wonder whether English people had the same sort of annual memorial ceremony for their poets as we did for ours. When I was a child, my grandfather and father used to take me to the Poets' Temple for the memorial ceremony twice a year, in Spring and Autumn. And again at the time when I held office as local governor of Tan-Tu district in An-Hui province, I had myself to lead people to the memorial ceremony twice in the year, in honour of the greatest poet of T'ang dynasty, Li P'o or Li Tai-P'o, whose name may be very familiar to anyone who has read some translations of Chinese poetry. It is said that he lived there with his uncle, who was the Governor of that district during a part of the T'ang time (AD 618–970). He was very fond of drink and most of his finest poems were composed 'in his cups.' A legendary story tells how he once tried to catch the moon in the river at Tsai-Shih-Chi and became an immortal in the heavens. Actually he was drowned. Then a memorial temple was built on the promontory of Tsai-Shih-Chi, where his clothes, discovered after his drowning, were buried in a tomb. His actual grave is in the family temple at Ching Mountain. We hold a memorial ceremony in those two temples, at the former in Springtime and at the latter in the Autumn. On these days all the men of letters gather together in the temple and the local authority leads the performance of the ceremony. It is open to the public. After the ceremony the members who took part in it have drink, food and all kinds of refreshments, which are provided by the authority. Some of them may paint and write poems for that occasion as well. When I conducted it in my year of office there I remember having written a couplet for the temple, which ran;

> Climbing up this high promontory,
> We wager for wine at Tsai-Shih-Chi;
> Madly whistling to the heavens,
> I dare not write a poem in the pavilion of this immortal.

But I know I am straying too far from the subject; I thought it interesting to compare the different customs of various countries. In this ceremony I have described there were manifestly displayed a love of poetry and of the poet. All these visitors had seen Dove Cottage and bought something as souvenir; I should like to know how deep was their impression of Wordsworth.

The guide book told me that this lake, with the exception of Rydal Water, was the smallest of all, and it was only one of the many natural ornaments in the beautiful valley; that was why Wordsworth made his home here, rather than by the shore of the most majestic lakes. I agreed with the comment, and was all the more eager to set eyes on the lake itself. I walked down to the lake side. My clothes were not so wet now and I could move about at ease. I looked at the summits of the high hills, their steep slopes, some thickly wooded and with swollen streams; my mind wandered to the poem on Grasmere by the poet. Though the hills around this lake were not unlike those of Buttermere, these were more richly forested, especially down below towards the valley. The sunshine pouring through the clouds changed all the colours suddenly and made the misty particles visible, and now the drizzling had stopped at last. It had one more beauty than Buttermere—a little island in the middle of the lake, of a bewitching and magical colour, purple and blue—and shining in the sun, at the moment when my eyes first fell on it. This island was unlike those in Windermere or Derwentwater, which were clothed with thick woods—it was but sparsely vegetated. I just walked on and on, telling myself that I should have to stay here for months before I could fully appreciate all that Wordsworth wrote in his poem of 'An Evening Walk':

> ... Where peace to Grasmere's lonely island leads,
> To willowy hedgerows, and to emerald meads;
> Leads to her bridge, rude church, and cottag'd ground,
> Her rocky sheep walks, and her woodland bounds;
>
> ... Sweet are the sounds that mingle from afar,
> Heard by calm lakes, as peeps the folding star,
> Where the duck dabbles 'mid the rustling sedge,
> And feeling pike starts from the water's edge,
> Or the swan stirs the reeds, his neck and bill
> Wetting, that drip upon the water still;
> And heron, as resounds the trodden shore,
> Shoots upwards, darting his long neck before.
> While, by the scene composed the breast subsides,
> Naught wakens or disturbs its tranquil tides.
> The song of mountain streams unheard by day,
> Now hardly heard, beguiles my homeward way.
> All air is, as the sleeping water still
> Listening th' aerial music of the hill.

As I walked and meditated, I suddenly found a large rock in my path, and there came into my mind the story of 'Mad Mi,' a well-known painter of the Sung dynasty, who once knelt down before a strangely shaped rock and saluted it as his brother. At this point I composed another poem:

> Lush green brushes against my clothes,
> Fresh is the mountain washed by rain.
> Stabbed by a shaft of the setting sun,
> Crystal clear is the water of the lake.
> Facing me there stands a lordly rock,
> To whom I bow in mockery of Mad Mi.

Then I noticed the time, already half-past six, and I had to catch the 'bus for Keswick in a few minutes. I felt profoundly sad to leave this beautiful spot, and I knew besides that I had soon to leave the whole Lake District as well. I grew thoughtful on my way to Keswick. After packing up my things and having supper, I went once more to Friar's Crag and again looked upon the evening mists around Derwentwater, and so took my farewell of them.

The next day I returned to London at five o'clock in the afternoon. I hardly can describe my feelings during that time before and after I left Lakeland. The past days had been a dream and not a dream. I would like to be dreaming for ever!

湖匯畫記

vii
Conclusion

*B*efore drawing a conclusion of my impressions on the Lakes, I should like to write down my poem 'On Leaving Lakeland':

In my native country, there is the Mountain Lu,
It rises too beside the P'o-Yang Lake.
And my home stands upon its shore,
All night, and day, I see the changing colour of the mountain.
I leave this lakeland, and with longing seek to return,
With some sadness thoughts are born of my distant home!

This was ultimately the chief feeling which I carried away from the Lake District, but I must admit that something deeper and more comprehensive would have taken its place had I been able to stay more than those meagre twelve days. I had not even had time to visit Coniston and Ullswater—the lake which is known as the 'English Lucerne'. And several of the others I had simply passed by with a glance from the 'bus. To pass a fair judgment upon the whole district one would have to see it in all seasons of the year and under all types of weather—to watch the changes under morning and evening light, in fine days, in snow, rain, wind. My comments here are both subjective and hasty.

You will have learnt from earlier pages that I am not one who finds surprises in Nature anywhere—wherever I am, in China or England, the forms of mountains, rocks, trees, streams, leave a similar impression on my mind, although a few superficial features may offer variation. Many a time while I stayed in the Lakes I felt myself back in my native country. The scene was constantly green, beautiful and peaceful, but the general appearance was no more *striking* in my eyes than a commonplace scene along the south bank of the Yangtze Valley—calm, undulating, agreeable. I hope my readers will not feel displeasure with this honest comment of mine; I am a Chinese, the native of a country rich in immense forms of mountain and water. I would grant power and lordliness to Scafell Pike, but on the whole those mountains and lakes were charming miniatures by comparison with some of ours. The English lakes leave nearly all their beauties open to the eye; little is cunningly concealed to give a fillip to the imagination. Many of our Chinese lakes are so vast that one's eye can reach neither end nor edge, while others of smaller compass have dykes, bridges, ornamental pavilions and so on built into their waters, to prove a constant diversion to the mind. I should pass the same comment on the hills; they are not only smaller in England, but also more open and never give one the impression of being far removed from towns and civilisation. If I lived in the Lake District I doubt that I should ever be able to throw off this urban feeling, due perhaps to the abundance of good motor roads and the quota of traffic which naturally accompanies them. But in China, if we say we are going to 'live in the mountains' it is a synonym for cutting oneself off completely from town life and all its amenities. My native Lu Mountain, for instance, is in its highest part three thousand eight hundred feet above sea level, and the people living at its foot have no notion of the lives carried on by the mountain-dwellers above them; there is a complete cleavage between the two types of living. And the people on the mountain seem like the mysterious inhabitants of a fairy land! This condition could hardly occur in the English Lakes—at least, such was my impression.

Among our lakes we have special delights, occupations, types of scenery, clearly defined according to the different seasons. In Spring we always go out to look at the pear and peach blossoms, which we are likely to find growing along the shores. In Summer these give place to lotus and water-lily floating on the lakes themselves, and in some places grow the charming water-caltrops. At sunset time swarms of little boats appear, which we call 'Picking-lotus-fruit-boats' or 'Picking-water-caltrop-boats' and are usually full of young girls who are employed for that work. The girls will be gaily dressed, and the general effect of the scene at that time in the evening is one of extreme charm. Very often they will lighten their occupation by singing. In Autumn nights we go out to catch the lake-crabs; while in Winter time, especially the early Winter, we shall see troops of fishing boats streaming out to fish in the dawn. The shape of the sailing boats and the colour of their sails make a varied and picturesque scene. My visit to the English Lakes whetted my appetite for returning to my native land; but, all the same, in one's short life it is good to have a taste of the whole world!

After all, I have been fortunate in being able to revisit my old friends, the mountains and lakes, though I must have seemed as strangely dressed to them as they to me. I was extremely happy with them, and am now only longing to renew my familiarity with them in the snow.

我鄉有廬山市
傍鄱湖側我家
湖之濱日夕看山
色歸去訂重游
悠然生遠憶

別湖口 必

In my native country, there is the Mountain Lu,
It rises too beside the P'o-Yang Lake.
And my home stands upon its shore,
All night, and day, I see the changing colour of the mountain.
I leave this lakeland, and with longing seek to return,
With some sadness thoughts are born of my distant home!

A Dream of the English Lakeland

CHIANG YEE

The English Lakeland has occupied my mind most of the time these days! How has that happened, I wonder? I do not know.

It seems that I have been wandering again in the valley of Wasdale Head. I noticed a difference from what I saw in summer time two years ago: I was not sure whether this was the same farm-house as before, but I could see neither the young girl who fed chickens with so much charm of manner, nor the cowherd who used to lead a group of cows out to grass and stared at my foreign face so inquisitively. There were even very few sheep seen eating and nibbling at grass among the hills!

It was cold; clear and calm in every sense. I walked along the same road from Wasdale Head to Wastwater. It was snowing, as you may imagine. Every bit of land seemed to be covered with a soft white blanket, although there were traces of footsteps along the road I walked. But clearly no motors had disturbed it yet. The cascading of the streams sent no powerful roaring into the ears, but just ting-tung, ting-tung, and ting-tung (sound of water drops) here and there; apparently most of them were frozen. I was smiling and frowning in turn, because I had so much on my mind at this time and my feeling towards the scenery was entirely in accordance with the change in my thoughts. Though, to be sure, the scenery had not changed in itself.

Then, I was standing by the side of Wastwater afterwards. It seemed strange to me that I had managed to find foothold at the bottom of the Screes, for the slope of it was very steep and descended straight into the lake. How could I stand there? I could not tell.

Soon, I felt some cold thing constantly touching my face, and then I noticed flake after flake of the snow flying towards me. Let no one think me greedy, that I opened my mouth so that those tiny white flakes could fly in as they liked. I thought I was taking part in some sort of magic, as the flakes of snow in different sizes kept blowing into my mouth, and many more pressed and flew about my body as if they were products of it. In such a quiet and cool state, everything seemed to be standing still, but actually there was a visible-and-invisible movement of a great mass going on. It was not my magic. It was the magic of Nature.

I lifted my head and cleared my eyes, trying to pierce through the thick cloud of snow flakes, now falling more and more densely. They were falling very slowly, some hanging about in the air for some time and some even floating sideways. In my mind and even in my sight, they were not snow flakes but swan's feathers. There might be an angel hiding in the clouds scattering down all these feathers, or the Russian dancer, Anna Pavlova, dancing 'Dying Swan' before mighty Nature and purposely letting the loose feathers drop from her dress. Suddenly a heavy wind came round from the side of Wasdale Head and made the snow fall down so rapidly, it seemed to form scores of white strings, no longer separate flakes. I thought they must be strings of a very old and mighty Greek harp, and even wished to play on it with my hands. Oh, this would not respond to my humble oriental hands, for I could play only my native Chinese instruments. There was so very little mist among the hills on both sides at this time, but the clear-cut outlines of the hills ranges or mountain-tops were indistinguishable from the sky, being almost the same colour, greyish white. The only great black spot was the surface of Wastwater, peaceful and calm to look on. And my own minute black shadow was of no account. What a different scene from what I had contemplated two years ago!

Then suddenly, I do not know by what means, I was standing along the Sty Head path. When I looked down the pathway, I saw most of the trees naked of covering, but some had white blossoms on their branches. Among them all, the pine needles stayed always green! I remembered I was once told some climbers liked to climb fells and rocks in Lakeland even in Winter time, and wondered why I saw none of them there that time. Perhaps they were on other mountain sides out of sight. I just walked on and on, and thoughts chased through my head in disorder. The more I thought, the more deeply was I bewildered. The longer I went on, the more I thought. Suddenly I realised I was on the top of Scafell. It was a miracle how I got there, as there seemed no easy way to the summit from Sty Head path. I hope my readers, if they are mountain climbers, will not ask me about the way I climbed, for actually I could not have climbed in their manner. By the time I reached the top, I was panting heavily. In one breath, I whispered to myself 'Oh, Mighty Nature!' gazing round all four sides. The fell or mountain tops below where I stood, and far into the distance, were all covered with snow, but I could still distinguish the curved outline of their ranges. I could think of nothing to say except once again, 'Oh, Mighty Nature!' Moreover, I paid my high tribute to the snow in the following form of a rhyme:

Oh my beloved snow,
How white and pure you are!

How deeply and earnestly is my heart with you!
You have hidden everything evil on earth,
You have given them new life,
I ask you to keep them white and pure always,
I beg you not to mind some minute spots on your
   surface.

Although you are made of such tiny and soft particles,
Yet you could change the hard and rough rocks beneath
   your arms.
After a time you will melt into nothing,
But you will return.

While I was murmuring these verses over and over, my mind went far away, and I seemed to be back on my native mountain Lu. I stood there as I was standing here. Here all was cool, calm and peaceful, and there was quietness there too, but with sadness and horror overhanging. The next instant, I was terrified by noises of aeroplanes and bursting bombs, and suddenly I was awake. Alas! it was entirely a dream! It was a dream of my beloved English Lakeland, but a misfortune it should have ended in such terror. It was lucky for me though to have woken then; I dare not think where the members of my family are now. Probably my English friends can hardly imagine the state of a Chinese mind in these days.

At the end of my small book *The Silent Traveller*, I described how extremely happy I was with the English Lakes and was only longing to renew my familiarity with them in the snow. Last winter I was busy with work, so I could not go. This winter I would not dare to go as I am afraid my mind would be drawn to strike the contrast between the peaceful English Lakeland and my dread native mountains and rivers. I have to thank Mr E. W. Hodge wholeheartedly for inviting me to stay with him if I would go to the Lakes again.

Before the winter came, I had thoughts of going to the lakes again if possible. After, my mind was filled with troubles, and my only desire about them was to meet them in my dreams. So it has happened! The invitation to attend the Annual Dinner of the Fell and Rock Climbing Club of the English Lake District from Mr Speaker might have started me dreaming. I enjoyed the dinner so much as I had the chance to hear more about the Lakes. Although my name 'The Silent Traveller' indicates that I could not talk, I would have recited some poems of mine on the Lakeland in Chinese if I had been feeling happier. I only hope my English friends have excused me this.

When I was in my native city, I used to recite aloud a poem one of our great poets, Su Tung-P'o, of Sung dynasty (AD 960–1276) on Lu mountain, which runs:

> Ridge after ridge and peak after peak there are;
> From afar or near-by, from above or below, each has a
>   different form.
> The true features of Lu Mountains cannot be recognised,
> Because we ourselves are always engulfed in these
>   mountains.

What more can I say about it now? I had better keep silent!

Having Climbed to the Topmost Peak of the Incense Burner Mountain

Up and up the Incense Burner Peak,
In my heart is stored what my ears and eyes perceived.
All the year—detained by office business,
Today at last I got a chance to go.
Grasping the creepers, I clung to dangerous rocks,
My hands and feet—weary with groping for hold.
There came with me three or four friends,
But two friends dared not go further.
At last we reached the topmost crest of the peak.
My eyes were blinded, my soul rocked and reeled.
The chasm beneath me—ten thousand feet;
The ground I stood on only a foot wide.
If you have not exhausted the scope of seeing and
    hearing,
How can you realise the wideness of the world?
The waters of the River looked narrow as a ribbon,
P'en Castle smaller than a man's fist,
How it clings, the dust of the world's halter!
It chokes my limbs: I cannot shake it away.
Thinking of retirement, I heaved an envious sigh,
Then, with lowered head, came back to the Ant's Nest.

From the original Chinese of Po Chü-I